The Empires Tour

Travel Through Europe,
With a Side of History

By

Wesley R. Mullen

Copyright © 2020 Wesley R. Mullen

All rights reserved.

ISBN:
ISBN-13: 978-1-4951-0306-3

Cover image by koorimidzu from Pixabay

THE EMPIRES TOUR

A WORD BEFORE DEPARTURE

The travels described in this book occurred in October of 2019 - months ahead of the outbreak of the Covid-19 virus, and in a time of more carefree journeys throughout Europe. My thoughts go out to everyone who has suffered through this pandemic - victims and their surviving loved ones. And I hope some day that we will all be able to travel about freely, when the streets will once more be teeming with the human activity described in this book.

Throughout this book, I have used the designations of BCE (Before Common Era) and CE (Common Era) in place of BC and AD respectively. This is not a concession to political correctness; it is an acceptance of the growing current usage of these designations.

INTRODUCTION: EPHESUS

1.

An early-morning haze hangs over the ruins of Ephesus. My wife and I trek along the marbled streets and view the remains of a Bronze-Age town that had flourished, in one form or another, for over a millennium. It was from this rugged terrain in Anatolia (today's Turkey), centuries before the city was established, that neolithic hunter-gatherers would make the journeys that would carry them to the Greek Isles. And it would be the descendants of these tribesmen who would return to build Ephesus. From this spot, I intend to follow the march of empires across Europe. Our cruise ship will carry us through the Aegean waters to the sites that I want to visit; from there, we will hopscotch around the continent to follow the civilizations that have shaped Europe and the world.

2.

The ruins of Ephesus stretch along a slow decline in the land, leading to a harbor area long since lost to sediment build-up. Tour buses drop travelers off at the top of the town, then make their way to the parking lot at the other side of the ruins. In this way, tourist throngs funnel down the paths at a leisurely pace as guides expound on the history and significance of the excavated city remains. As the morning haze lifts, stone buildings and columns that had been obscured in the mist come into stark relief, revealing the extensive archeological work that is still ongoing.

John Turtle Wood, a British architect, was the first digger in the region to attempt to find the fabled Temple of Artemis in 1863. He only discovered the pavement of the temple, and interest in the region waned until German archeologist Otto Benndorf, in 1895, began excavations in earnest. The archeological work has continued ever since.

As we walk along the smooth marble path, our guide points out the various ruins that a century of manual labor and scholarly study has exposed. With the haze gone, a landscape of stone arches, bare columns, and half-cleared walls announces the huge expanse of the town that ancient Greeks, pushing out the Persians and reclaiming lost coastal towns in Anatolia, had built in the 10th century BCE. The city's timeline is a history of Greek dominance constantly interrupted by conquest: in 650, the Cimmerians razed the town; rebuilt, it was conquered in 560 by the Lydians and then by the Persians before falling to the Greeks again around 479 BCE.

After Alexander the Great died, Ephesus was ruled by one of the three generals who divided Alexander's empire amongst themselves.

3.

Ephesus, as befits a town of its age, is a treasure trove of architectural styles. Netting and pre-fab structures set up by the current clutch of archeologists around the area tend to mar the historical feel of the place, but they have uncovered a wealth of riches both in physical finds and in additions to the historical record. Greek and Roman styles predominate, for when Rome entered an area, little stood in its path to conquest. So it is that the gentle downward slope of our walk brings us to the city's most famous - and most photographed - structure: a Roman architectural masterpiece called the Library of Celsus.

The Library was originally planned as a funeral monument for a proconsul named, of course, Celsus. But the sheer size of the building soon lent itself to the founding of a library that rivaled the one in Alexandria in Egypt. Unfortunately, the building collapsed in 262 CE, with only the façade surviving; and that portion of the building fell to an earthquake a few centuries later. Only in the 1970s was the façade restored - rebuilt, for the most part, with the original stones.

And there it stands, overlooking the rest of Ephesus and

dwarfing the tourists who stand at its entrance steps and gaze with awe at this colossal feat of architecture. Two levels of massively high columns and arches loom over onlookers. Groups gather and snap photographs; selfies are taken by the dozens; and professional photographers, weaving through the crowd like sharks sizing up their prey, take pictures that, through the modern wonder of digital imaging, will be waiting at the exit to the buses to lure those who want the "perfect" memory of their visit.

4.

As we head toward the exit where our bus awaits us, we pass a large section of ground that is currently being excavated. While it is too early to determine what the ruins signify, the layout - with its grid-like appearance - reminds me of a town market. As Ephesus continues to be uncovered, the magnitude of the city's size at its height is also being revealed. This city thrived under Rome's supervision, and became the Eastern Roman Empire's most important center after Constantinople.

But the loss of its harbor - and the loss of trade that followed - marked the start of a downward spiral as the populace moved from the city. Attacks by Arab tribes, and natural disasters such as earthquakes, accelerated the process; and by the 15th century, Ephesus was abandoned and lost to the world until German and Austrian archeologists began to uncover it at the end of the 19th century.

We have one more stop to make; but from the port of Kusadasi, 19 miles to the south, our ship will carry us to the same islands that the ancient Anatolians from this region had sailed to as they sparked the rise to empire that would define the development of Europe for centuries to come.

5.

The art of haggling is a finely-honed skill that favors the local merchant, who lives and breathes this craft every day as he sells to novice and experienced travelers. The seller knows his wares and he knows the prices that he will offer and that he will accept. He is the consummate salesman; the shop is both his battlefield and his boardroom, where he will negotiate terms that leave both sides feeling as though they are walking away victorious. But the merchant knows better.

Aladdin's Rug Warehouse lies a short distance from Ephesus. Guides will bring their charges directly from the tour of the ruins to the shop, where weary feet can rest, free beverages are offered, and the show will begin. And what a presentation it is!

Years of practice have turned the workers into expert showmen; and the performance that they put on is an art form of darting motions and unfurling carpets that is breathtaking to watch. As a manager describes each rug - noting its beauty and the materials (wool, cotton, or silk) that have gone into it - as it appears, two other workers roll out the finished product in a wonderfully choreographed display that highlights the carpet's appearance without obscuring a single rug that has come before.

The result is a kaleidoscope of colors and designs that clash only enough to display the uniqueness of each piece. Perhaps a half-hour has elapsed, and a couple dozen rugs have been geometrically lined up, before the spell is broken as the manager concludes his descriptions and invites his audience to remove their shoes and to walk on the carpets to feel the luxury that owning one of these pieces will bring.

Then the salesmen move in, taking individuals aside with the mastery of a predator separating his prey from the herd. It is a ritual that is understood by both seller and potential buyer - this is the way of things. Our salesman is Hamdullah Akin, a gentle-spoken man who helps us to zero in on the carpet that we so terribly need for our home office. We would meet him again when he came to the States and personally delivered our rug, and we spent a few hours together discussing politics, friendship, and other non-rug-related topics.

Haggling, as I noted, is an art; and the time for negotiations is upon us. In this arena, Mr. Akin holds the advantage; we have just recently been instructed in the necessity to bargain over the price of everything in this area of the Mediterranean. It is as if Mr. Akin is playing three-dimensional chess, and we are asking, "How does this horsey piece move, again?" Thankfully, we are able to reach an arrangement that feels fair to all of us; and we return to the tour bus the proud possessors of a gorgeous blue-and-white woven masterpiece.

THE GREEK ISLES

1.

While the whole of Europe lay fallow, the seeds of empire were making their way across the Aegean Sea. Anatolian seafarers from what is now southwestern Turkey were sailing to a small group of islands to the west, where they would establish a culture that united them with mainland Greeks seeking a more arable soil for farming. The union would produce Europe's first proto-empire: the Cycladic civilization, noted today for their figurines carved from the islands' marble. As skilled sailors, they operated their coastal settlements as stopover-points for sea-going traders.

Today, they are still stopovers on the cruise routes that

bring thousands of tourists to their shores, where travel has become the primary industry - in some cases, such as Mykonos, the only industry.

2.

The Aegean Sea has, without doubt, the bluest waters that I have ever seen. Standing on the deck of our ship as we approach Mykonos in the late afternoon, the deep hues wrap around us as the prow cuts through the sea and we enter the harbor.

In another life, in the fourth millennium BCE, I would have faced the challenge of striking out from Anatolia in a wooden boat - the first of many explorers who would dare adventure to continue the populating of the earth. Mingling with small groups who ventured from the Greek mainland, the newly established culture would form their own unique identities on each island; but common threads would bind them so closely that Christos Tsountas, a Greek archeologist, could label them, in 1899, as the Cycladic civilization - a chain of islands that circled, or *cycled around*, the sacred isle of Delos (more imaginative souls would suggest that the chain got its name from its most popular mythological resident - the Cyclops).

But in 2019 CE, I am too old to hire a slow boat to experience a rough journey on the water; my wife also would have objected to us hauling our luggage onto a fishing vessel, noting that time was playing a factor in our voyage. Not being a fan of cruise ships - transportation is a means, ultimately, of getting from point A to point B - we nonetheless decide that such a vessel would serve to get us to our destinations with comfort and speed.

By the late afternoon of our first day at sea, we are docking at the city of Mykonos, on the island of Mykonos

(I know. But…it's *their* town and *their* island, so…).

3.

Mykonos Town hugs the beach as it curves around the harbor. *Chora* (literally Greek for "the town" - used, we are told, when a town and the island that it's on have the same name) gleams in the late afternoon sun; its narrow, cobbled streets are hemmed-in by white-washed buildings. Most structures are only two to three levels high, with cafés and shops occupying the ground floors; as evening falls, lights appear in the upper windows as families gather, throwing blocks of light onto the walls directly opposite. Bright lamps shine in the store entrances, highlighting souvenirs and Greek crafts as travelers pass.

Tourism has become the main - and, it would seem, the only - industry of this most cosmopolitan town of the Cyclades islands. It wasn't always so. Centuries ago, while still major stopover ports for Mediterranean traders, Mykonos and her sister islands provided materials for other industries that fueled the ancient world. This isle's main contribution was flour - ground in its windmills and packaged for shipment throughout the known world at the time.

Mykonos also owed its preeminence in the Aegean to its proximity to Delos, a sacred island that had been inhabited centuries before the Anatolians and Greek Ionians arrived. Mythological deities had reportedly been spawned on Delos; and it retained its spiritual importance through the ages, eventually becoming a tourist attraction in its own right. Day tours still leave Mykonos for the smaller island, with some travelers electing to stay for the duration of their vacations.

As night falls, more street lamps produce an aura of claustrophobic, winding passageways. Church steeples of white stone shine as the glow of electric lights creeps up the buildings, dwarfing the surrounding homes. And moments later, we emerge at the far end of the harbor, where, at Chora's edge, a line of four windmills - white with darkened roofs - is lit by spotlights on one side and by the red-tinged sky on the other. Cameras click, lights flash - and unforgettable images are created by the fleeting sunset for travelers to carry as memories of the island's powerful beauty.

Now the procession back to the other end of the harbor - and the shuttle bus awaiting us - begins, as the scant light sources across the broad stretch of ground separating the smaller streets from the beach make our footing less secure. We learn later that one of our fellow passengers has fallen and broken her arm and elbow in four places; a helicopter airlifts her that evening to an Athens hospital. It is a harbinger of things to come, as I will discover in Athens - a reminder that danger can lurk even in the most recreational forms of travel.

It is a long walk along the harbor which nevertheless seems short in duration as we listen to the muffled sounds of celebration from restaurants and cafés.

4.

It is perhaps fatuousness on my part that I generally loathe cruise ships, yet here I am sailing in comfort across the Aegean Sea. With the exception of trolleys and trains, I regard transportation as merely a means of getting to a destination - *that's* where the adventure begins. I'm waiting for the day that *Star Trek*-style transporters are the rage, and I can eliminate those interminable hours spent inside a metal tube thousands of feet in the air.

But Connie deserves comfort time after months of recovery from surgery; and I want to experience, even in truncated form, plowing through the waters that ancient Anatolians navigated in more dire conditions to move ever more westward in the Mediterranean. And so we endure the creep of hours as we dart past smaller islands, heading to our next port.

Somewhere on board, elderly compatriots are being "entertained" by activities geared toward a view of Americans as the "Beverly Hillbillies in Europe." Connie and I enjoy lunch in one of the ballrooms, while she has a beer and I indulge my taste for rosé wine.

Back in our cabin, I edit the photographs that I've taken so far. We stroll up to the pool area and order another drink. And suddenly, the word sweeps across the ship like a rolling wave that we are minutes away from the next port of call.

5.

"An island made by Gods for people" is how the Mykonos website describes their home; but if gods created that island, they didn't stop there. The sea is dotted by their work, and little Patmos has an outsized reputation as the Island of the Apocalypse due to the presence of St. John on their shores.

During their time under the Roman Empire, Patmos became a place of exile; and in 95 CE, the apostle John arrived. During his two-year stay, he wrote the book of Revelations in the Cave of the Apocalypse, just a short distance from the Grotto of the Apocalypse (I'm sensing a theme). Today, the island trades heavily on John's story, running tours from Skala, the commercial port that hosts all cruise ships. Connie and I pass on the tours, and walk the streets closest to the harbor.

Patmos is one of two islands we will visit where passengers must take a smaller boat, or "tender," to be put on shore. As with so many ports in the Greek isles, the town sits on a crescent-shaped harbor and reaches up the hillside behind it. As we stroll along the narrow streets - pedestrian walkways, really - we notice that, as familiar as the general features are (white-washed walls, contrasting roofs, brightly-colored shutters and doors), there is a uniqueness that pervades the town. It is the same on each island that we visit. Every isle hints so subtly "yes, we all share a related culture, but *our* island is special because...," and we feel the difference without being able to speak it aloud.

We stop at a café along the harbor and sip some wine. The October wind off of the water is comfortably warm.

Tenders wait at a wharf to return us to our ship.

6.

Many of the islands have named their capital city after the island itself: Mykonos on Mykonos, Patmos on Patmos - the lack of imagination is appalling. But the remedy is just as maddening. On such islands, the residents rename (or perhaps, "rebrand" is a better word) such towns Chora - literally, "the town." So now, instead of asking, "Is that Mykonos the town, or Mykonos the island?", you can simply say, "We're going to Chora."

But is that Chora on Mykonos, or Chora on Patmos, or Chora on…? Fortunately, some ships disgorge their passengers in a port town other than the capital. So, on Patmos, we set foot in Skala. When we arrive at the island of Rhodes, we will go ashore at…Skala. Skala is apparently the Greek word for "the port."

Soon we will disembark at our next stop, in Chora…or Skala…or Skala…or….

My brain hurts.

7.

If the Greek Isles had a historical capital, it would be Rhodes. One of the largest islands, its centuries of political importance and its wealth of architectural structures warrant a full-day stop on our cruise. And one of the perks of using a Greek cruise line is their brilliant decision to employ at each location local tour guides who are also archeologists.

Homer notes that Rhodes sent warriors to Troy. Minoan, Mycenaean, and Persian emperors recognized the strategic importance of Rhodes, as each conquered the island in succession. So too did Alexander the Great. And in the Middle Ages, the Knights Hospitaller made Rhodes one of their strongholds; even today, it is known as "The Island of the Knights."

To those of us who love history, a day on this island is like walking on hallowed ground, as the dust of centuries stirs beneath our feet. Our first outing is to the city of Lindos, about an hour from the harbor. The narrow streets teem with shops and cafés as we trudge upwards toward the town's Acropolis. It is a brutal climb, as the steep incline combines with the surge of tourists wending their way up and down the stone streets and stairs to make the lung-pounding hike. An occasional stop to catch our breath gives us stunning views not only of the white-walled city below, but the winding streets that we have just maneuvered; covered in spots by white sheets strung between buildings to deflect the morning sun, they resemble small tunnels bracketed by shops.

By the time that we reach the base of the Acropolis, only to find another set of ascending stairs, Connie and I have to admit defeat; and for the first and only time during our trip, we give in to exhaustion and wish our fellow travelers good luck as we turn back.

A few steps down and we see what we had been too winded to notice on our way up: donkeys, saddled and waiting with their owners, ready to transport human cargo. So tempting! - but our minds are functioning on such a basic level that all we can think about is putting one foot before the other until we have descended to where our bus awaits.

Later in the day, we venture through the Medieval Old Town of Rhodes, with its fortifications and ever-present gift shops; then the harbor beckons, and dusk brings a familiar muted rumbling of tourists and merchants across the waterfront.

8.

"That ship has sailed" takes on new meaning for the Greek Isles in October. Cruise ships are making their last departures from the islands as the season ends; for the next five months, sea tours will be reduced drastically, and with them, the huge tourist trade that fuels the local economies. Individuals may make day trips by ferry from Athens; some may even stay for a few days before heading back to the mainland. But now, as October fades into

November, the merchants must push their wares - rugs, mugs, and other souvenirs and crafts - with a single-minded focus of depleting their inventory before a lull that will last until April of the following year.

Tourists will now go on a shopping frenzy of unparalleled proportions. They know that the economics of haggling are on *their* side. Like sharks, they will circle the stalls and shops. Merchants will push forward their remaining stock, like throwing so much chum in the water; they know something that most of their customers do not.

In an average season, over a thousand cruise ships will stop in harbors throughout the islands. But the last couple of years have been lean, and this year - 2019 - only about 300 ships have landed. A Kurdish merchant near Ephesus in Turkey informed us about this downturn, and Connie and I make good use of it in our purchases.

Now, as dusk falls on the island of Rhodes, potential disaster strikes: a looming storm sends a bolt of lightning that knocks out the electricity in the town of Rhodes. Shops are plunged into darkness, with only their outer shelves visible in the fading daylight. Merchants scramble to assist customers, while ensuring that gifts and trinkets do not "disappear" into the oncoming night.

Connie and I make our way to the harbor, and our ship. Barring a quick resolution to the problem, Rhodes is in for a long night - no place to be stranded in those darkened streets.

9.

The royal-blue domes that top the white-washed exteriors of Oía's churches are the island of Santorini's most iconic image. But given how sadly few of those buildings we actually see, the most captivating sight is the water-filled crater below - the collapsed remains of a volcanic eruption that destroyed most of the island and helped to bring about another empire's fall.

Some 3600 years ago, that eruption left the remains of Thera (Santorini's original name) anchored in the southern Aegean Sea like a huge question mark; but there is no question that, with Mykonos, this isle is one of the most popular stops for tourists. Cruise ships cannot dock at the waterfront, so tenders are used to ferry visitors to shore. From the ship, we can see caravans of tour buses weaving up the cliff face behind the wharf. The dizzying ascent winds back-and-forth, with hairpin turns at each end of a length of inclining road with no barriers. As we approach land, the stark realization that *that* will shortly be *us* sinks in. Once ashore, we are moved swiftly to keep us from thinking too much about what we are about to do with our lives. The buses start their upward trajectory; the resulting views are incredible and terrifying; the hairpin turns are nerve-fraying.

Once above, we head north to the city of Oía. Circumventing the capital city of Thera, the bus rolls through a rocky landscape, until the first blue domes appear on the skyline ahead. If we were expecting to ride the famous donkeys or the cable cars to a summit, we are sadly mistaken. That experience occurs in Thera.; over the years, the attractions of the two cities have come to intermingle in the popular imagination. We proceed on foot. Upwards toward the main square, we see our first blue-domed church up close as we reach the summit. When we stand looking down at the gleaming caldera, the sight of our massive ship as a small blot on the water staggers us.

The town exudes a comfortable vibe that invites us to stroll along its streets and to descent the white stone steps (everything, it seems, is white here except those roofs) to cafés and patios that will face the setting sun as dusk falls. Then, in semi-darkness, we make our way back to the bus, drive toward the harbor, and - Mother of God! - roll down that heart-stopping cliff face.

As the tender heads back to the ship, I could swear that I hear prayers being offered in muffled voices - and one of those voices is mine.

10.

The Cycladic culture didn't end so much as it folded into the Cretan civilization that flourished through another influx of Anatolians and Greeks from the mainland and the Cyclades themselves. Artifacts from the islands would be found in numerous places around southern Europe, long after the travel industry transformed the isles; the hordes now descending on the Aegean Sea are tourists, and their monetary contributions continue to inject new life into the area.

KNOSSOS (CRETE)

1.

Puttering about the flea markets of Athens in 1893, archeologist Arthur Evans chanced upon seal-stones that contained symbols that he could not decipher. The markings on these pocket-sized gemstones, which Evans called Linear A, led him, over the years, to the island of Crete. There, in the early 1900s, he uncovered Europe's first empire. Calling the culture the Minoan civilization, after the mythological king Minos, Evans' excavations revealed Knossos, one of several ancient palace-cities across Crete.

Without the use of military might, the Minoans established the first sea empire in Europe. With no need for a standing army, their massive naval fleet struck out to control trading routes throughout the Mediterranean, from Sicily in the west to the Levant in the east and from the Greek isles south to Egypt. Their outposts became trade centers along the various coasts.

2.

We approach Crete over the same waters that had brought a second wave of Anatolians from Asia Minor along with Greeks from the mainland. These settlers mingled with the original Neolithic inhabitants of the island, and by 3000 BCE, the Minoan civilization had emerged. Throughout the next millennium, they would extend their sea empire, seeding aspects of their culture throughout the Mediterranean and influencing the region long after their empire fell. Copper and tin - materials necessary for the production of the metal that gave the Bronze Age its name - were their stock-in-trade. So skilled and efficient were Minoan sailors that surrounding countries would hire them to transport their goods between third parties.

By 2000 BCE, the Minoans were reaching the peak of their prosperity, and a period of intense palace-building began across Crete.

3.

We sail into the harbor of Heraklion in the early

morning hours. The city, in its earliest incarnation, had been a port for the palace-city of Knossos; it would only be officially established as a town in the 9th century CE. After a light breakfast, buses take us to the archeological dig that is still uncovering the palace.

The dig's entrance is an unimpressive opening between large bushes on one side of a narrow lane. By comparison, the line of shops on the other side, catering to arriving tourists, is in-your-face imposing, commanding visitors to stroll through the buildings either before or after walking through the ruins.

Once inside the palace grounds, however, the vista opens onto a monumental project that is still exposing the once-massive palace-city that dominated the island. Knossos was not so much a royal building as it was a colossal city - the center of finance, religion, government, and culture for the local Minoans. It is estimated that between 40,000 and 100,000 people occupied the grounds at any given time. So it is no wonder that archeologists continue to explore and discover structures throughout the dig.

There is a clearly marked path, and an equally controlled flow of humanity as busloads of tourists wend their way around the grounds. Again, for those of us with an enduring love for history and for the ongoing discovery of ancient civilizations, places like Knossos instill an overwhelming sense of awe - for the achievements of the cultures, for the sheer breath of their empires at their heights, and for the influences that snowballed into other cultures and that still resonate through the world's civilizations.

We move through the ruins as though we are cogs on an assembly line. As our guide imparts her knowledge of the Minoans, my mind is elsewhere, soaking in not only the beauty of this place, but its significance to future empires that we will encounter during our travels. The linear A language - which defies translation even today - will, for example, lead directly to another language: linear B, which will form the basis for classical Greek, as that culture comes into its own.

As we near the end of the tour - over an hour later, as just the uncovered ruins and walls are spread over almost 40 acres - we come to Knossos' most iconic sight: the restored northern entrance to the palace. From the remaining base, three massive bright-red columns support a thick roof with round white circles or disks surrounding its exterior. Beyond the columns is the colorful relief of a bull - the symbol of Minoan might. Along the uncovered end of the base, two partial, broken red columns reach uselessly up. The whole structure just hints at the greatness of the culture, surrounded by the ruins that symbolize its fall.

4.

Ah, the shops opposite the palace of Knossos! We came, we saw, we bought. The less said of this, the better.

5.

We head back to Heraklion.

In the 15th century BCE, the volcano that formed the island of Santorini erupted, with cataclysmic results for the Minoans. Although the primary ash plume went away from Crete, the eruption precipitated other natural disasters for the island, including earthquakes and a massive tsunami that battered the coast and destroyed the port of Heraklion. Despite some restorative work by conquering Romans, it would be six centuries before the town would be rebuilt and become the capital of the Emirate of Crete.

Parking less than a mile from the harbor, our guide turns us loose on the older part of the town. A short walk brings us to Lions Square. Dominated by a large fountain in the center decorated with four lions, each looking in a different direction, the square is surrounded by shops and cafés. Just one street over is a stunning example of the influence of Venetian dominance of the island from 1204 until 1645: a massive administrative building featuring a style of covered external corridor called "loggia." It's a visual surprise, standing amidst the lower, decidedly Greek architecture of the square and its surrounding streets.

One of those streets leads us down a busy pedestrian cobblestoned lane flanked by gift and craft shops on either side. At the end of the road, before emptying onto the harbor, sits a small café where Connie and I relax with a midday wine. The sun is casting an oppressive heat over the city, and the awning that shades the tables and seats offers little relief. We finish our drinks, then head to the ship.

6.

That volcanic eruption on Santorini did more than batter Crete's coastal towns. Massive earthquakes and spreading ash clouds damaged Minoan outposts and disrupted trade routes throughout the Mediterranean, leading to a decline of the civilization over the following decades. Weakened prey attracts predators, and - its outposts open to attack - it was not long before Crete fell, probably to the Mycenaeans - the early Greek warriors that Homer wrote about in <u>The Iliad</u>.

But Minoan culture did not disappear. Outposts throughout the Mediterranean retained their influences; and the Mycenaeans adapted much of what they found on Crete into their own culture, which, in turn, would find its way into the classic Greek civilization that followed them.

Mainland Greece beckons us.

ATHENS

1.

Around 1100 BCE, the Mycenaeans discovered what the Minoans before them had tragically learned that aging empires, weakened over time, will fall to new ambitious cultures. No one is certain from which direction destruction came upon the Mycenaeans - from the Sea Peoples, the Phoenicians, a group known as the Dorians - but their collapse ushered in a Greek Dark Ages that spread throughout the eastern Mediterranean, effectively ending the Later Bronze Age.

When the region emerged from this cultural slump, around 800 BCE, the Greek mainland had settled into a system of city-states (*poleis*). A united Greek empire, in the purest sense of the word, never actually existed; a loose collection of city-states , each autonomous yet capable in times of danger of forming short alliances, populated the land. Each city-state would come into prominence in its turn, giving rise to an Iron-Age Greek civilization - an empire of intellect and ideology that would eventually influence the entire southern Mediterranean.

That "empire" came to be identified with one city in particular: Athens.

2.

We dock at Piraeus.

By 800 BCE, the three deep-water harbors that formed the port had enabled and paralleled the rise of Athens as a significant *polei*. A commercial port at the time, and 8 miles southwest of Athens, the site is now a thriving suburb of the city and home for arriving and departing cruise ships and local ferries.

A crush of humanity pushes out from the port terminals. Spilling into parking lots and harbor sidewalks, arriving travelers now vie for taxis, buses, and Ubers. Kostas swiftly snakes his taxi to the curb in front of us, and moments later we are headed for our hotel.

We speak no Greek, and Kostas has only a smattering of English at his command; but in a thirty-minute drive through winding streets, we are able to hold a kind of friendly halting conversation. He is solidly built, but not overly large, and probably in his late thirties to early forties; an image of Anthony Quinn as Zorba the Greek pops into my head as I reimagine him these many months later.

By the time that we reach the Athenian Callirhoe Hotel, Kostas has convinced us to let him take us down the coast in a few days to visit the Temple of Poseidon at Cape Sounion.

3.

Towering above Athens is the Acropolis, a colossal outcropping of rock that dominates the city sprawled below it. The Mycenaeans utilized it as a fortress to occupy the high ground in case of attack, and subsequent rulers of the region continued that practice. By the mid-5th century BCE, however, with the city expanding beneath and around it, and with a period of relative peace and prosperity falling upon the "empire of Athens," the Acropolis became the focus of religious devotion (and, in particular, of the city's patron goddess Athena).

This is the moment when Athens truly came into her own - a period of almost a century now referred to as the Golden Age of Athens. A city leader during that time, Pericles, directed the building of its most iconic image: the Parthenon - Athena's temple on earth - at the Acropolis' summit. Other structures were erected on the broad plateau; and the flowering of classical art, architecture, literature, philosophy, medicine, and other disciplines that flowed from the region would lead to the "Greek civilization" that we are taught about today in our schools.

We quickly drop our luggage at the hotel, and make the Acropolis our first objective. By mid-morning, we are standing at the base of the plateau.

4.

We look up - straight up - at the Parthenon looming over us. Photographs do no justice to the sheer height of the Acropolis, and I feel myself go a bit weak in the knees as I gaze upward.

"I won't make it to the top."

The words blurt out even as the adrenaline pumps me to make the effort. After all, this is one of the main reasons for coming to Athens: to visit the site walked by Plato and Aristotle, by Mycenaeans and Persians, by Alexander the Great, by Ottoman Turks…. And Cicero's words ring in my ears: "Wherever we go in this city, we seem to be stepping on a piece of history."

As I start forward, I feel Connie's arm wrap into mine; we walk along the gentle slope leading past some trees and onto the sun-drenched path of gravel and stone. Our journey to the top will be slow and steady, the passage at a surprisingly comfortable incline and with built-in stops: pausing at the edge of an ancient amphitheater or perching atop a set of steps leading down to broken arches through which to photograph a receding Athens below.

There are small guardhouses that serve as first-aid stations at various spots along the climb. As we pass the last one, I am surprised to see how close we are to the massive columned entrance to the plateau. It has taken us an hour to get here; in fifteen minutes, we should be entering the Acropolis grounds. I turn and tell my wife to watch her step as we ascend, then I trip on an outcropping of rock and go full-face forward and down into the stone.

5.

I see and feel the brim of my hat hitting and curling

against the ground, slightly cushioning the blow; at the same time, I seem to feel my beard softening the impact to my chin. My nose and glasses take the full brunt of the fall. It is a slow-motion ballet of brutality, all the more remarkable as I am caught totally unaware by the sudden drop. How can two such feelings co-exist: slow-motion rapidity?

All that registers is the intense pain on my face, and the certainty in my mind that I must have broken my nose. Then my body reports pain along my arms and legs. In a dazed stupor, I am aware that I am rolling over onto my back, pushing off with my hands. And then other hands appear - dozens of hands, and I realize that several people have put their arms around me and are lifting me to a standing position. Still dazed, I cannot make out faces. Several people are pouring bottled water over napkins and wiping my face and hands clean of grit and blood. To my left, I'm aware that Connie is holding my arm.

Down to the last first-aid station we go, my feet barely touching the ground as people pass me along. From the station, a Red Cross unit is called down from its location on the Acropolis; and as I wait, all that I can think of is how close to the top we are, and - damn it! - I *am not* going down without getting to the Parthenon first. The unit arrives. Two young nurses approach; and while most older men may imagine how wonderful it would be to have two attractive women fawning over them, the fact is that having one's face scrubbed of blood and ingrained gravel with antibacterial wipes - followed by a smearing of orange-hued tincture - is a rude reconnect with reality.

After what seems an eternity, Connie and I are allowed to continue our trek up to the Parthenon.

6.

Atop the crest of the Acropolis, on the southern side, I gaze down at Athens. Somewhere below me, blocked from view by a stand of trees near the base, is the new Acropolis Museum. Beyond that is our hotel, and, continuing southwest, that hazy area on the horizon is the port of Piraeus. My wife is on the other side of the Parthenon, awaiting the start of festivities set to commemorate the 75th anniversary of Greece's independence from the Nazis in 1944.

I move to my left and look east towards Hadrian's Gate on the streets below. Another section I want to explore, Plaka, also lies beneath my feet between the Gate and the Acropolis. The north side of the plateau is off-limits this morning, as politicians and military officials await the opening of the ceremony that will also feature folk dancing and a boys' choir recital. Were I able to view the city from there, I would be looking down at Monastiraki, the old town flea market. I mentally mark the locations.

I am Zeus, looking down from Mount Olympus, at the world below. That is the intoxicating feeling that fills me as I realize that I can view the entire city of Athens from above. No other city has ever revealed itself so completely and openly to me from such a vantage point. Yes, the Eiffel Tower may show me views of Paris; and the Riesenrad Giant Ferris Wheel may lay much of Vienna at my feet. But only here does a city's geography and history lie below me in its sweep of colliding civilizations; no other city seems to unite, so seamlessly, the architectural evidence of its various rulers - ancient Myceneaen, Greek, Roman, and Byzantine - with traditional Greek structures and modern museums and apartment buildings.

But it is not enough to see the city from above. I descend to the streets, and explore.

7.

At ground level, the blending of architectural styles looks even more seamless than it appears from above - and for good reason. Within a century of Athens' "golden age," it was once again just one of many city-states vying for supremacy; this time, however, it was an external force that would conquer and unite the Greek mainland. Phillip II of Macedon and his son Alexander the Great swept through the peninsula, eventually creating a massive empire that stretched from the Balkans to western India. Greece was united for the first time; and that unity would spell its downfall.

With Alexander's death, the western portion of his empire went to one of his generals. Later, as the Roman Empire expanded to the east, Greece lay open for the taking: a unified Greece proved easier to defeat than several dozens of city-states all requiring military campaigns. But this is where it gets tricky.

The Romans had a passionate love-hate relationship with the Greek civilization. Almost from the moment of first contact between the two cultures, Romans were enamored of the tremendous achievements of the Greeks: their art, their architecture, their philosophies and literature, and their mythology. So great was their admiration, that they slavishly copied those Greek accomplishments in Rome itself and in their subsequent settlements. Even the Greek gods were Romanized: Zeus became Jove, Poseidon became Neptune.... So it is no surprise that Greek and Roman architecture sometimes feels almost indistinguishable.

The problem was that Greeks were just, well…Greeks, not Romans. If you were not Roman, you were inferior - so how could you admire work by such sub-Roman people. The answer, of course, was that the Greeks would "become" Romans by virtue of their inclusion into the empire. Time would blur any other inconvenient inconsistencies.

8.

Those who have traveled with me know that my first-day ritual, whenever I arrive in a new city, is to search out and ride on the local Hop-on Hop-off Bus. These tour vehicles invariably wend their way knowingly through the boulevards and side streets of a city to its most important and most touristy (many times the same) sites. These 90-minute-or-so rides (usually done non-stop for the first time) are key to my nailing down a mental map of a place, positioning points that I want to explore and giving me a perspective on the scale of my journeys - a more practical way of judging distances in a city than by guesstimating from a map.

So we amble down from the Acropolis, from gravel paths to a wooded area separating the cliff base from the road. As we pause in the shade, an elderly man greets me and asks if I remember him. My mind furiously races through possibilities, but I draw a blank. He senses my embarrassment, and tells me that he is one of the people who had pulled me up after my fall on the hill. I sheepishly confess that the moment was a blur of confusion, but I thank him profusely for his aid. It is a gentle reminder that good people are always in our lives, even as you stumble through a fog of events.

Below the Acropolis, we board the double-decker bus,

filling the afternoon with an elevated view of Athens. As we proceed, the Parthenon looms above us like the hub of a wheel, letting us know which side of the city we are traveling through at any given moment.

Shortly after, we walk back to our hotel, our appetites pushing us to its top floor.

9.

The hotel restaurant provides a stunning view of the Acropolis, bathed in orange rays as the sun starts to set behind it. Soon, floodlights will bathe a darkening Parthenon against a deep royal blue sky just before darkness envelops the plateau, leaving only shadows to dance along the stone columns.

I am beginning to truly learn the limitations of my doctor's orders against eating meat. On the cruise ship, a lavish buffet menu ensured that the seafood and pasta possibilities would slake my appetite; in the more austere selections provided on a hotel menu, my choices are… sparse. Gone are the days when I could wander off the main tourist lanes, find a small restaurant on a side street, and order blindly from a menu with no English translations - true culinary exploration that led to more pleasant surprises than I had a right to expect.

Now I have to work within the restrictions of my treatment, and that means knowing exactly what I'm eating. So: salmon, baked whitefish, and penne pasta until I can find a touristy eatery with English listings of… anything else.

10.

The October sun casts a mild heat in the early morning. Having eaten a light breakfast, Connie and I decide to walk from the hotel to Hadrian's Gate. The path takes us past the Acropolis base and over to Amalias Avenue - a 20-minute stroll that invigorates us in the gentle sunlight, and leaves us staring up at a relic of the Roman occupation of Greece.

And here, that subtle similarity between Greek and Roman architecture is on full display. Beyond the gate, a few hundred yards across a dirt field, sits the Temple of Olympian Zeus - or, at least, what remains of it. Built between the 6th-century BCE and the 2nd-century CE, during the period of Athens' prominence, the Temple was pillaged by barbarians in 267 CE; only twelve columns survive. But they are massive remnants, and their similarity to the Roman-built Hadrian's gate, raised around 132 CE, is striking.

The rectangular gate itself is all that remains of a larger structure now long gone. But its two-level arch, with its second-tier columns, still commands the gentle curve of the major thoroughfare passing before it. And moving back slightly into the dirt field, I am able to get a perfect photograph from a low angle looking up through the bottom arch that frames the Acropolis looking down in the distance.

11.

On the far side of the Acropolis from our hotel lies Monastiraki, the old-town flea market. It may even have been in one of these shops, in 1893, that Arthur Evans first stumbled upon the relics that led him to uncover the Minoan civilization. Fanning out from Monastiraki Square in every direction, narrow lanes lead visitors through a maze of storefronts that are barely cubbyholes; crowded paths squeeze buyers in and out of the shops like toothpaste being squished into a myriad of nooks and crannies.

Connie and I alight from a bus onto the square. To the left, the Church of the Pantanassa borders the large paved plaza; ahead, the ever-present Parthenon sits in the distance, overlooking the market. We pick a lane at random, and find ourselves wandering through an eclectic collection of booths featuring leather goods, tee-shirts, souvenir trinkets and magnets, musical instruments (mostly string), and just about any other combination of goods that can be imagined.

One group of items dominates the market; in fact, we will find these products throughout Athens and, later, Istanbul. There seems to be a great affinity for board games, specifically backgammon and chess. Entire shops are devoted to these wooden and metal works, and the craftsmanship is exquisite. Chess sets, especially, are prominently displayed throughout the market: the size and variety of their pieces - from kings to pawns - are endless, and provide the craftsmen with a greater range of styles to work on than do backgammon pieces.

And then we happen upon a modern miracle that saves the entire trip for me. Since my fall at the Acropolis, my glasses have set askew my face. For over a day, these twisted eyepieces have triggered my obsessive-compulsive disorder; if I could twist my own face to match the contours of these misshappened shafts of plastic and glass, I would. Now, suddenly, we stand before a display of sunglasses, and Connie suggests that I ask for assistance with my problem (in truth, she probably would have shoved me inside just to see if she could prevent me from continuing to adjust my face).

Inside, a young lady behind the counter takes my glasses, and, in a series of twists that I can only describe as heart-stopping, she readjusts the frames and puts them back on my face. Stunned by the suddenness of her actions, it takes a moment to dawn on me that, for the first time in my life, my glasses fit perfectly. I let it sink in: perfectly! As I sputter my thanks, she refuses to take any payment; but as God is my witness, that girl has missed her true calling.

As we recross the square to get a bus, I look at Connie with a broad grin and proclaim, "I can see! I can see!" She shakes her head and mutters, "Oh, please."

12.

And then there are the museums.

Whatever shard of antiquity is not displayed on the streets of Athens has found its way into one of the multitude of museums that dot the city. So, despite my propensity for roaming the streets and cafés of Athens while viewing archeological ruins, I decide early in our stay to visit at least two institutions: the National Archeological Museum and the New Acropolis Museum.

The New Acropolis Museum, which opened in 2009 CE at the southern base of the Acropolis (replacing the original that had occupied the plateau with the Parthenon), is that happy combination of museum and archeological dig that satisfies my desires both to study and to experience. The very modern building, packed tastefully with artifacts uncovered over the centuries in the surrounding area, sits atop an active dig site; the unique design of the plate-glass first floor allows visitors inside the museum to walk several feet above the ruins that are being currently excavated. It is a truly surreal moment as we watch the walls and pottery and narrow passageways open below our feet, with a glass ramp carrying us away from the dig to a more traditional second floor.

While not nearly as high as the Acropolis, the views of Athens afforded from the top floor are evocative of the city's blend of ancient and modern architecture.

North of the Acropolis, we arrive at the National Archeological Museum just after midday. This much more traditional institution will occupy our afternoon, as a carefully-designed progression of halls guides us through archeological wonders age by age. Here we see the handicraft of the Cycladic and Mycenaean cultures; our walk takes us past treasures from all areas of Greek civilization - from Sparta, Corinth, Delphi, and, of course, Athens.

In one of the first halls, I stop and stare at an artifact that I have only seen in photographs and documentaries: the Mask of Agamemnon. I am stunned; it is more breathtaking than I could ever have anticipated. Behind the glass, the gold death-mask glistens and demands an audience for its artistic and historical heritage. Could this really be the face of the Mycenaean king who led his country against the city of Troy? It *should* be: it is proud and fierce, the ideal Greek warrior-king.

After what seems like an eternity, I feel Connie tugging at my sleeve. There are other sights to see - so many objects, so little time. Hours later, we emerge into the fading sunlight. For the first time, I am reluctant to leave a museum to return to the streets.

***

13.

Souvenirs? We don't need no stinkin' souvenirs! After all, *we* are not common tourists. We may pick up a magnet or two from each city, but…we're explorers - travelers through ancient lands and capital towns, soaking up the history, culture, and…oh my Lord, just look at this shop! In the shadow of the Acropolis, on the way back to our hotel, is a corner property whose windows are chock-a-block filled with statuettes, busts, small pottery pieces of such exquisite craftsmanship that we can feel our resolve melting before the enticing works that overload our senses.

This is Zophoros, a souvenir shop that wraps itself around the meeting of Veikou and Hatzihristov Streets. Entering from a front door that faces diagonally into the intersection, we see the store extending along each street, expanding the interior of a store somehow artfully clogged with the widest variety of items that we have seen, or will see, during our time in Athens.

Time ceases to exist. Beautifully carved statuettes - seemingly created from sleek marble, but probably a more common polished stone - line shelves both against the windows and along narrow paths through the shop. Small busts - Homer, Socrates, Leonidas (the tourism industry has learned to profit from Hollywood's vision of ancient Greece - *300*) - fill in smaller gaps in the shelves. We look, we collect (statues and busts and chess sets, oh my! - and, yes, magnets), and we lay our swag at the counter of the store owner, a brusque but kindly older gentleman who informs us that he ships merchandise to all sorts of clients around the world. With that, we pay and leave our purchases with him to send to our address in the States.

So, there will be no lugging of souvenirs from city to city. Our gear remains mobile and light - much, I'm afraid, as our bank account is becoming.

14.

True to his word, Kostas and his cab are waiting for us in front of the hotel. It is early morning, and he aims to beat the work traffic out of Athens and to get us to Cape Sounion by 9:30 AM. He flies through the streets and we have suddenly left the urban capital behind, traveling southeast along the coast road.

Not quite half way to the cape, Kostas pulls off the road and heads into a small park at Vouliagmeni Lake (literally, "Sunken Lake"). The oblong lagoon is bordered on one side by a lawn that looks as if an artist has carefully applied the brightest shade of green to the grass that I have ever seen, and on the other side by the massive cliff face of Mount Hymettus. Where the rock meets the lake, large caves open, letting warm water running through underwater caverns into the lagoon - creating the perfect spa conditions that have blessed the area since the 19th century.

We have arrived before any other visitors, so we can take in the natural beauty of the spot as the cool morning air brushes through the park. In a while, bathers and kayakers will descend upon the scene; the kayaks will find their ways to the darkened cave entrances and venture inside. But they will only go so far, for no human has managed to completely explore the vast caverns, even though several have died trying over the years.

We drive farther southeast, and around 70 miles out of Athens, we arrive at Cape Sounion and the Temple of Poseidon. Homer first mentions Sounion in his <u>Odyssey</u>; but it is during Pericles' reign and the Golden Age of Athens (in the late 440s BCE) that the temple is built. No surprise that it looks like a smaller version of the Parthenon: Pericles himself directed the construction of both structures. Time and barbarian pillaging have taken their tolls on the temple; the roof and elaborate interior designs are, as at their sister temple in Athens, long gone. But standing at the top of a promontory surrounded on three sides by the sea, and bathed in the pure light of the morning sun, the Temple of Poseidon is a monolithic marvel that struts its architectural beauty and its honored place in the history of Greek civilization.

We trek leisurely up to the temple. We have arrived before the crowds; only a handful of visitors stroll atop the cliff. Later, we descend to where Kostas is waiting for us, and share drinks as we toast his country's place in history. Then we head north, to the Athens airport, where we will hop countries and empires as we continue to pursue the flow of civilizations through Europe.

ROME

1.

Rome presents the classic trajectory for the rise and fall of an empire: a soup-to-nuts extravaganza of foundation, expansion, over-expansion, and decline. While Anatolians were sailing the Aegean Sea to form the first European civilizations, Rome's ancestors were just emerging from the Eurasian steppes and heading into eastern Europe. By sometime after 1500 BCE, a group known as the Latins had turned south into the Italian peninsula and eventually settled on the eastern bank of the Tiber River.

Mud huts went up along the seven hills that formed a protective shell for the tribes; population growth drew them together as a community and then as a village. From huts to wood shelters to stone buildings, by 753 BCE, Rome was a town with a name and a growing reputation. Heavily influenced by the Etruscan culture in nearby Tuscany, the genius of Rome lay in its ability to absorb the practices of "foreign" cultures while steadfastly retaining their own unique identity.

This chameleon-like skill made the Roman takeover of central and southern Italy feel like a natural flowing force that simply absorbed the surrounding lands. Conquered tribes and states were allowed to continue governing with their native institutions and leaders, as long as they acknowledged being under Rome's protection.

And so the Roman Republic grew, organically and rapidly.

2.

I mucked it up this time. Usually, I will book a hotel within the town center - by my definition, the area of a city that contains the historical and cultural sites that I want to see (also by my definition, that part of the city that sits within the loops of the Hop-on Hop-off Bus). Rome Central is the area ringed by a circle beginning at the Vatican on the Tiber's west bank and extending north to the Villa Borghese, then around past the Trevi Fountain and the Colosseum, and closing at its starting point. And try as I may, I could not get affordable quarters anywhere in that region. It wouldn't take long to discover why.

The morning rain stops as we reach the outside of the airport terminal; and after our usual new-city-do-we-get-a-bus-or-a-taxi-to-the-hotel argument, we hop into a cab - I win! - and head into Rome. I can hear Connie's sharp intakes of breath as our driver navigates the overcrowded streets; it's like a huge bumper-car riot - without the bumping. Roman motorists must be born with an innate sense of space and distances. Our taxi slips between cars, trucks, and the occasional pedestrian with a sinewy motion that defies the laws of physics; I don't think that I can get a breath of air to fit between us and the cars that parallel us.

I can tell that our driver is getting mightily annoyed at us. We have traversed the width of Rome, and we are still some distance from our lodgings. Farther east, we make a few quick turns, and we are suddenly at the Best Western Globus. Our bags are quickly unloaded; and even though our driver gives us his card in case we need another ride, he is speeding out of the neighborhood before I can thank him.

As we mount the hotel steps, I look around. The area is an older commercial set of streets, but its age is leavened by the presence of dozens of university students buzzing through the lanes as they head to classes in the surrounding schools. A block away, a Metro station opens onto a line that we will learn takes us directly to the Colosseum. So maybe I didn't screw up too badly.

3.

The Metro exit across from the Colosseum shudders as it expels hundreds of sweaty passengers from its bowels onto the street, adding to an already chaotic clash of tourists and residents. I am back in Rome for the first time in forty years, and the difference is stunning. I have never seen the sheer mass of humanity clogging the streets the way that I find it now. Yes, the city has always drawn a phenomenal number of travelers; but the whole world seems to have converged on this metropolis this year, stymying traffic and making a trek through the city an endurance sport.

As we reach street level, the Colosseum rises ahead of us, and, to the right, the Forum begins its broken stretch across the city. At the height of the Republic, in the first centuries BCE, this entire area would have been a solid mass of marble temples, columns, arches, and roads; now ruins fight for the right to remain standing and, hopefully, to be restored. The Forum steadfastly holds its position, as if challenging the city to displace it or, worse, to disrespect and ignore the history that it represents. Tourists are its lifeblood: their constant flow provides both the interest and the income that will preserve the crumbling structures.

Elsewhere, the various monuments' fates are bleaker. In the Dark Ages that followed Rome's eventual fall, the city was looted and left in disrepair. With the Renaissance, new architectural styles filled the empty fields and crumbling ruins. Unlike Athens, where styles blend with a natural flow of age and era, Rome's choppy collection of architectural designs makes the urbanscape a challenge to follow. Tall Roman columns sit majestically in tufts of ground between medieval buildings, which themselves may be facing an 18th-century monument or a modern office building.

Ancient Rome hangs on, barely.

4.

As if to punctuate the ancient world's fierce determination to be preserved, the Temple of Hercules Victor majestically stands hemmed in on three sides by multi-lane roads that roar with traffic. Just east of the Tiber River, this circular building is the oldest marble structure in Rome, and the city's oldest surviving Greek marble work. Over the centuries, it has gone from being a flea market to a temple to a church; and it has lost its roof - the current tile roof was a recent restoration. But it persists, trapped by the surrounding modernity.

Towering over us at 35 feet, we circle the temple. Given its pedigree, it seems the logical place to start our travels through the winding streets. A brisk walk along the Tiber, then a short trek toward the Pantheon is interrupted as we arrive at Largo di Torre Argentina - symbolically, the end of the Roman Republic. In the late 1920s CE, while demolishing an old neighborhood to erect new buildings, workers stumbled upon one of the most important archeological finds in history. Ringed now on three sides by roads and on the fourth side by a broad sidewalk, the dig sits a few dozen feet below street level: ruins of four temples, with roofless columns reaching above the surrounding lanes, now lie verdant as grass retakes the grounds.

And here, on the Ides of March in 44 BCE, Julius Caesar was assassinated. The pride of the ancient world, the Roman Republic, had expanded beyond the capacity for senatorial rule, and glory-seeking generals like Caesar were vying to fill the growing power void. The Republic slid inexorably into a Roman Empire. But it went with a fight: Caesar's death was an ill-fated attempt to retain senatorial control over Rome and her territories; his great-nephew, Octavian, would soon become sole head of the government, and, as Augustus, would usher in another 400 years of Roman dominance in the west.

All of these facts rush in on me as I stare at the broken walls and overgrown lawns lying quietly with their history below me. Like standing on a battlefield, I am aware of the swirl of destiny that has played out before me: a singular spot that marks a turning point in western history, that will take Rome - and the world - down a new path that will forge new empires and shape cultures throughout Europe.

A furtive move below shakes me from my thoughts, and brings me back to the present. Cats are scurrying about the dig; the ruins now serve as a shelter for dozens of feral felines. A sadness descends. I am sure that Connie, with her love of animals, is heartened by the refuge; but I find the overrunning of such a historical site to be hugely depressing.

5.

The Republic may have died, but the move to throw up massive and more impressive buildings was just getting started. Augustus would ensure that Rome remained the focus of the civilized world; and his successors were no slouches when it came to erecting monumental tributes to their own conquests and achievements. As early emperors fell into disrepute, their statues and temples toppled with them. A new emperor would raise his own monuments.

Rome is a procession of building, destruction, and rebuilding. Sometimes, one era built over another; other times, one era of arches and columns went up side by side with another, as if in competition for the ages. And, dwarfed by the size of these achievements, travelers are left in bewilderment of their place in time at any given site. There are no straight lines, nor concentric circles, that lead orderly through Roman architectural history. A walk through Rome is a dazzling journey from one era to another: turn from Trajan's Column (113 CE) and gaze upon the Victor Emmanuel II National Monument (1885-1935 CE), then walk a few blocks to the Largo di Torre Argentina (44BCE). From there.... The city is a massive puzzle of architectural and historical sites - a delightful puzzle, but a conundrum nonetheless.

Connie and I opt for a series of small, one-hour focused guided tours. Over a period of a few days, these guides navigate us through a maze of side streets, cutting from one location to another while framing a particular time period. Using this method, we can run our journeys along a thread that walks us through a sharpened view of Rome's history.

Along the way, we enter the Piazza Navona, a 15th-century example of Baroque architecture in an open-air plaza that covers the Stadium of Domitian (an oval-shaped chariot racetrack built in 80 CE). While swirling with humanity, the crowds are nowhere near as congested as in other parts of the city; a warm, dry breeze flows through the long pedestrian oval, and residents and tourists alike take the moment to pause, sit by one of the fountains, take a relaxing breath, and stroll on before returning to the clogged arteries of Rome Central.

6.

Respite from a grueling midday sun means finding shelter in one of the hundreds of cafés and restaurants just off of the Tiber, and indulging in an hour or two of hearty eating. Each day, we pick a spot at random (as long as they have a multi-language menu), forego the outdoor tables under the colorful awnings, and slip into the soothing ambiance that substitutes cool wall tiles and a light breeze for the sweaty alternative of an outside seat.

Salmon with pasta reigns supreme in my culinary choices, with slight change-ups in sauces and side veggies. Connie's tastes are somewhat more permissive; and though she expresses guilt for eating meat dishes before me, I wave away the objection. Just looking at some of the steak and veal and poultry creations set before her is enough to delight the gourmand inside me. These meals are minor masterpieces in inexpensive culinary design and practicality: feasts as much for the eyes as for the taste buds.

We do not attack these dishes. We savor every aspect of the experience, from the rosé wine to the main course, to the bread and oil that fills the gaps in our stomachs between servings of fish or meat. We opt for a light dessert, enjoy another drink, and venture back out into the sunlit streets. Wine and a full belly, it seems, are a fine, if temporary, sunscreen.

7.

After lunch one day, a short bus ride presents strikingly different views of Rome. As we digest our meals, we sit atop our vehicle as it rolls through the Villa Borghese; the park is a lush expanse of manicured lawns and marble structures, with a lake filled with couples rowing boats under the shade of the trees. We thread our way through a narrow arch and reemerge into a modern landscape.

The Empires Tour

The road widens into a winding boulevard with sharp curves and the glitter of a cosmopolitan avenue in mid-afternoon. On one side sits a staid embassy exterior; on the other is the Hard Rock Café, and then both sides explode with upscale shops and outdoor cafés as we twist and turn along the road in a downward spiral toward a wide piazza.

And that fast, we are once again in the midst of an architectural Rome predominated now by works commissioned by emperors Trajan and Hadrian. After the Julio-Claudian line (Augustus to Nero) played itself out, emperors generally rose from the ranks of the generals. In 83 CE, Trajan took the throne, and by the end of his reign had pushed the empire to its fullest extent. From Britain in the north to Egypt in the south, from Spain in the west to the Middle East, Trajan's empire became the canvas for a massive building spree of stunning temples, arches, and monuments.

Hadrian, Trajan's successor in 117 CE, continued the building process both in Rome and in the provinces (most notably Greece). Hadrian's focus as emperor was to consolidate the existing empire and to fortify its boundaries. This period represents the apex of the Roman Empire, and the colossal number of architectural wonders from this time are the key structures that continue to draw travelers to the city every year.

Hadrian's rule of the empire also coincides with the first losses of territory for Rome: Mesopotamia and Armenia in the east were ceded to the Parthians as Hadrian realized that the empire had become overextended.

8.

A new morning draws us to Rome Central. This time, I want to visit a specific site: the Trevi Fountain. In 1977 and again in 1979, I had strolled almost by accident into the small plaza that barely contained the incredible fountain. Gleaming marble and gushing waters seemed to drench the surrounding grounds with brilliant light and cooling mist. The pooled water at the fountain base shimmered with a light green hue, probably as a result of a painted marble bottom; the whole of the front was ringed by people walking along the fountain edge tossing coins into the water and hoping that Fate would return them to Rome someday.

This particular morning, Connie and I find our way to the plaza by coming down a side street that winds from somewhere behind the fountain and enters the area on the right side of the massive sculpture. And my heart sinks, for this plaza is a moving carpet of humanity covering every inch of pavement. A railing now rings the pool of water, allowing only limited access to the mass that threatens to lurch into the fountain with each shift of the human eddy that roils about the square.

The fountain itself remains a monumental masterpiece; it has been restored at least twice in the last two decades. But the plaza is as choked by tourists as the streets and passages of the rest of the city this year. From a small perch at the side, I take some photos; then Connie and I somehow make our way through the crowd (or maybe with it) to the closest street, where we retreat down a narrow lane to find an intimate café for lunch. Inside, we watch the press of tourists flow past as we order a simple meal of pasta and shrimp - and wine.

* * *

9.

Allowing time to digest our meal, we take a secondary loop of the local Hop-on Hop-off bus and head out of Rome and along the Appian Way to the Catacombs of San Sebastiano. About fifteen minutes from the city, the catacombs draw large crowds; the resulting tours, grouped by language, are tightly controlled to keep visitors moving through the cool but claustrophobic tunnels.

Pausing to look at the small basilica of the church directly ahead of us, we turn right to the ticket office and enter a small display area that serves as gathering point for the trip to follow. Our guide arrives and cautions us to stay close together as we weave through the subterranean passageways, then leads us down a steep set of stairs. The guides know these caves intimately, and the maze that greets us is familiar territory for them.

As we walk, we sense, rather than feel, the almost imperceptible downward slope of the tunnels. An occasional swelling gives us a momentary impression of rising, but then we are gently passed down to lower levels. Crypts and ossuaries nestle into the sides of the caves, providing permanent rest for dozens of unidentified martyrs. Periodically, we come suddenly into a broad chamber, where the guide gathers us to impart information about the site. We usually arrive at these "rooms" just as another tour is leaving; given that we never see a group walking ahead of us, but hear voices from adjoining tunnels, I suspect that each guide has his own personalized route, each converging on these larger chambers.

Now we go deeper. The walls close in slightly, as if the original builders decided to move more quickly and less carefully with their work. Connie and I are both short in stature, but I notice that some of our fellow travelers are stooping slightly to protect their heads. Our shoulders just brush the walls, and movement slows as we navigate the sharper turns that take us, thankfully, to the next open chamber. As the guide proceeds, we can feel a general unrest flowing through the group as they react to the possibility of even tighter passages.

But then we are rising, a slight incline sensed against the bottom of our shoes. Shortly, we come into a small antechamber, from which a steep flight of stone steps leads us to a brightly-lit hall that doubles as a subterranean repository for Christian artifacts. Here, the guide concludes his tour with remarks about how St. Peter was believed to be buried in these catacombs before his remains were reburied where St. Peter's Basilica now stands; he also suggests that St. Paul was interred here, though the historical record is vague on that point.

One more flight of steps, and we are entering, from the far side, the church that we viewed on our arrival. Half an hour later, we alight from the bus beside the Circus Maximus. The faintest sound of racing chariots plays in my head as I view the desolate dirt oval. An empire's decay greets us on our last afternoon in Rome.

10.

Early in the day, before we fight our way through traffic to the airport, there is one last spot that I must visit: the Pantheon. In three previous visits to Rome, I have never stopped by this structure; now it strikes me as the perfect analogy for the rise and fall and rebirth of the city.

Constructed as a temple during Augustus' reign, its ruins were built over by Trajan and Hadrian as a new temple whose basic form survives to this day. Later, it would be converted into a Catholic church, and that would be its salvation. While Roman citizens would quarry the Colosseum for stones to use for makeshift stone huts during the Dark Ages, the Pantheon remained largely untouched as Christians carried a vibrant faith through treacherous eras. With the dawn of the Renaissance, the domed structure anchored a new wave of architecture and artistic achievement.

Our arrival at the site reminds me of my first glimpse of the Trevi Fountain over forty years ago. Winding through small streets, we first see the front portico: massive Corinthian columns support a pediment over the stone patio leading to a set of huge doors. As Connie and I get closer, a small square opens up before the building. Hat respectfully removed, I pass into the vestibule and then beyond to stand under the stunning concrete dome. There is an oculus, an open circle, at the top, which provides one of the two sources of natural light in the Pantheon. It floods the interior, picking up the flickering tongues of fire in the candles throughout the church.

We feel the slight decline of the floor; rain water that enters the church through the oculus drains down into a subterranean system that disposes of the runoff. The floor is patterned with squares that unevenly cause a feeling of unease as we weave our way about the crowd. Large patches of people congregate and move as a single organism under the dome, and all eyes are directed upward with arms extended to snap photos. We are a pod of targets ripe for plucking, as pickpockets and other thieves maneuver through the human mass. Connie carries no outer accessories, and I keep everything I carry in a cross-chest bag; we navigate the clogged floors with little fear. But I wonder how many of our fellow travelers are going to exit the church suddenly realizing that they have been relieved of their wallets, purses, and other possessions - quite a few, from the faces that I am seeing as we pass through the square.

11.

The Roman Empire lasted for a thousand years. During that time, it was eventually divided into the Western Roman Empire and the Eastern Roman Empire - one empire too large to be controlled by one leader, with dual emperors each ruling one half of the whole. But only one emperor would hold supreme power, and eventually Constantine took over as sole ruler. Over the ruins of the Greek city-state of Byzantion, he built a new city: Constantinople, the New Rome. After his death, the empire split again: a Latin-speaking but weakened west, and a Greek-speaking, thriving east.

While Constantinople was ideally positioned to rule the Eastern Roman Empire, Rome became a liability when it came to fending off barbarian attacks from the Germanic tribes or the Frankish forces of Gaul. Western emperors took to using mobile capitals as threats arose from different sides of the empire - to no avail. By 410 CE, Rome was sacked; in 478, it succumbed to the latest wave of assaults and the last western emperor was deposed.

Did the Roman Empire fall? Residents of Constantinople would argue that point with you. Although we refer to a Byzantine Empire today, those people would steadfastly insist that they were Romans still living in a Roman Empire. The evolution to a new nation-state would be a slow but inexorably steady process. And Connie and I were following that passage of empire to its next flowering of glory: Constantinople, known for the past several centuries as Istanbul.

VATICAN CITY

VATICAN CITY

1.

Another empire was growing within Rome, an empire that would match and then surpass the growth of its host throughout the Mediterranean: the Christian Church. Not a kingdom of lands and men, this was an empire of faith and spirit, an empire of souls. But it would come to influence kings and princes, and it would intwine itself deeply enough into the affairs of man to ensure its continued existence over millennia.

Augustus was Rome's emperor when Jesus of Nazareth was born; his successor, Tiberius, ruled during the time of

Jesus' ministry and death. Neither knew of these events in a backwater territory of the empire, nor could they imagine how an obscure Jewish sect could one day piggyback on Rome's expansion to convert its citizens. Once Peter the Apostle arrived in Rome as a prisoner, and Paul of Tarsus had opened the sect to non-Jews (without the requirement for rituals such as circumcision), the new religion took root.

Through years of acceptance and of persecution, the Christian faith spread along the very roads that Rome built to connect the farthest-flung regions of its rule. While the pope remained in Rome, missionaries traveled to the outer reaches of Britain, Spain, Asia Minor, and past the empire's boundaries to Germanic tribes along the Rhine. Long before the barbarian hordes emigrating from the east overran Rome, they themselves had already submitted to the Christian faith.

By the 4th century CE, Emperor Constantine had declared Christianity the official religion of the Roman Empire, and Old St. Peter's Basilica (over which the present-day basilica of the same name is built) became the residence of Peter's successors.

2.

As we stroll west from the Tiber, the boulevard before us opens onto St. Peter's Square and to a vision iconic to millions of Catholics: St. Peter's Basilica. Catching our eyes first is the large obelisk in the square's center, an Egyptian artifact that supposedly was originally situated near the place of St. Peter's death. During the Renaissance, when the current basilica was built, it was placed in the piazza as a "witness" to Peter's martyrdom; now it faces the supposed site of Peter's burial.

Wrapped around each side of the piazza, in curved arches ending before the boulevard, is a double-tiered colonnade that funnels visitors into the basilica doors. But we're looking for another way in. Through the colonnade and down a back street, we turn west again to reach the rear of the Vatican. There, we join a group that has access to the nation-state literally through the back door. We have arrived at the Vatican Museums.

Seven buildings house 54 galleries holding some of the world's greatest art and sculptures, and feature works by Raphael, Leonardo daVinci, Michelangelo, and others. We are almost giddy at the prospect of seeing some of these masterpieces; our guide is an encyclopedia of all things Vatican. But the press of humanity is claustrophobically tight in the narrow, cramped hallways that form the galleries; they are the streets of Rome magnified a dozen fold.

Despite the close quarters and occasional blasts of body odor, we push through the halls for the next few hours. The crowd dwindles only slightly when we leave the main galleries and step into side rooms; but this allows us to view, for example, Raphael's Rooms, a set of parlors displaying the works of one of the Renaissance's greatest artists. *The Coronation of Charlemagne* and *The School of Athens* are incomparably beautiful when seen in person instead of on a printed page. I feel humbled. I may never achieve perfection like this in my writing, but just gazing upon such artistry is, at the same time, frustrating and inspiring.

3.

I find myself unusually restless as we approach the final gallery: the Sistine Chapel. Forty-plus years have played havoc with my memories; but I still remember the awe that struck me, at the age of sixteen, when I saw Michelangelo's work. I was certainly no fan of art - then or now - but the staggering size and beauty of the accomplishment affected me in a way that I found perplexing. It seemed as if the artist himself was reaching across an immensity of time to tell me what I could achieve if I devoted my life to my passion. And that passion was, and is, writing. The seed was planted; it would take decades to find the particular niche that would drive me to produce the works that give me the most pride and joy.

Now Connie and I enter the Chapel, it seems to me, from a different direction than years earlier, and suddenly the room seems smaller - more compact - than I recall. I realize that things can look larger to young minds, but the contrast here is jarring. Nonetheless, the ceiling, over a hushed crowd of observers, is magnificent in its scope and colors. The hand of God touches Adam, and the room seems to radiate illumination from that central point. We gaze upward; we study the images that the artist has so gracefully created. The writer in me is ashamed as I think, "There are no words...."

4.

After Constantine's death, the Roman Empire broke again into a western and an eastern half; the Christian church separated along the same fault line. Although the schism wasn't official until 1054 CE, the eastern church adopted the Greek language; the western church, now the Roman Catholic Church, adopted Latin for its rituals and ceremonies. Roman popes were on their own now, and they devised a survival plan designed to benefit both the church and the secular monarchs who were coming into power.

It was a simple reciprocal deal: the church would confirm that the particular monarch of a territory was chosen - anointed - by God (thereby giving him legitimacy among his subjects); in exchange, that king would guarantee the protection of the church and of its supremacy over the souls of his people.

By the dawn of the Renaissance, the Roman Catholic Church held most of the lands of central Italy. These Papal States would be ruled by popes who were also military leaders. The most famous was Julius II, the Warrior Pope. He was equal parts soldier, scholar, and diplomat, and in the first decade of the 16th century, pushed his territory to its maximum expanse. He also commissioned the Sistine Chapel and the other Vatican Museums.

Over the next few centuries, the Papal States would shrink in size until, by 1870, only the Catholic enclave in Rome remained. That same year, Italy was unified as a sovereign nation. Still, while it may have lost physical territory, the empire of souls had flourished and spread worldwide.

In 1929, Vatican City was established as a sovereign state.

5.

Our tour of the Vatican Museums ends with our entry into St. Peter's Basilica. A huge, ornate nave stretches before us, leading to the central dome; natural illumination floods the areas beneath, as people mill respectfully toward the light. Connie and I turn to the right immediately after entering, and walk to the north aisle.

There, one of Michelangelo's masterpieces stands behind an unbreakable glass enclosure: the *Pietà*. I first saw it in 1967; today, the gleaming marble statue of the crucified Jesus lying across his mother's lap, her right arm supporting the upper half of his dead body, is still moving. Philistine that I may be, works like these connect with me through their creators; I am standing at one end of a time portal that allows me to "see" Michelangelo. Think of it as a form of "history feeling," the same emotions I feel when I'm standing before the tombs of George Washington or Vasco da Gama. In this instance, it is the act of creation that unites me with Michelangelo (or any of the other painters and sculptors whose works we are seeing today). His presence before me provokes a feeling of kinship; his artistry drives me to better my own work.

In 1967, I was able to approach it without barriers and to easily photograph it. In the intervening years, vandals have necessitated the glass precautions that separate viewers from statuary; the gentle light illuminating it helps to defuse reflections for present-day photographers.

A half-century before Julius II, Pope Nicholas V commissioned the building of the current basilica. He authorized the demolition of the Colosseum; the damage inflicted to the arena in the Dark Ages was compounded with the removal of enough stone to build the basilica's foundation, leaving the Colosseum the shattered hulk visited by thousands of travelers today.

Nicholas also authorized the selling of indulgences to raise construction money, a decision that would come back to ravage the church and his successors. One of those, Pope Alexander VI, commissioned Michelangelo to create the *Pietà* in 1498.

After another hour or so of strolling through the church with no particular plan other than to let the opulence of the place overwhelm our senses, Connie and I move out into St. Peter's Square - paradoxically quieter and calmer despite the city sounds after the intense murmuring hush of the faithful inside the basilica. As we head to a late lunch on the other side of the Tiber, the secular world engulfs us again.

ISTANBUL

1.

Disregarding months of warnings from our

family and friends to avoid Turkey, Connie and I now find ourselves in the bustling city of Istanbul - and a more stunning or enjoyable stop on our itinerary I cannot imagine! I will try, as adequately as I can, to put into words the dizzying mix of feelings - of western familiarity and eastern "alienness" - that rush upon us as we experience what I *knew* would be the high point of our journey, yet never realized would captivate us so completely.

As the historical center of our tour of empires, Istanbul was always a must-see destination: hub or capital of at least three civilizations that spanned over two millennia, this city represented the pinnacle not only of empire, but of art, architecture, philosophy, and science. But we had not anticipated the sheer beauty and appeal of this bi-continental metropolis nor of her people. The western influences that anchor us in the "reality" that we know are constantly being altered delightfully by the "alien" eastern influences that open our eyes and minds to a different view of life and living. The result is not just a study of the past, but a modern exploration of a very living, thrilling city.

Modern Istanbul sprawls across the Bosporus, claiming a home in Europe and in Asia. The Asian side, with the exception of a palace or two, is the residential face of the city; on the European side, an inlet of the Bosporus (the Golden Horn) separates the northern and southern halves of the city. North of the Golden Horn lies the business center and the modern facade of the metropolis. Here, skyscrapers proclaim the city's 21st-century status, while wide boulevards display trendy shops sharing sidewalk space with the omnipresent MacDonalds, KFC, Burger King, and Starbucks.

South of the Horn lies the Old Town, the beating

heart of the city. Set on a peninsula, this ground has been tamed by ancient civilizations since 660 BCE, when Greeks built the city-state of Byzantion. One of the last polities to gain prominence at the height of Greek culture, it fell to the Romans in the first century CE. Emperor Constantine the Great built his New Rome over the Greek ruins and made the city the capital of his empire. Constantinople became the new center of the world.

2.

Mesut is the man! The concierge's role in the fine-tuned running of a hotel and in the lives of those under his care is sadly underrated in today's world. It is he, behind the vast machinations that seem to keep an establishment running, who holds the threads that allow the imperceptible humming of the busmen, elevators, waiters, kitchen, and cleaning crew to smoothly interact with guests unobtrusively throughout the hotel.

And at the Antea Palace Hotel, it is Mesut who greets Connie and I warmly as we pass through the wood-and-glass-paneled doors. The lobby is intimate and tastefully decadent. The afternoon sun is quietly threatening to dip below the horizon, but light still bathes the hotel fixtures and the austere armchairs where we are directed. Mesut sits down at his desk, radiating confidence and friendliness.

After some pleasantries are exchanged, Connie is given a cup of coffee, while I get a small glass of tea. Moments later, I realize that we have been checked into the hotel, with a smoothness that puts to shame any other hotel's front desk. We sip our drinks, and Mesut proceeds to set us up for the next few days with guides and tours that will ensure that we see the essential Istanbul. I am sure that the final choice was left to us, but all I seem to recall now is that we are suddenly on our way up to our room with all arrangements made.

3.

Open windows allow the cool evening breeze to sweep gently through our room. We have almost two hours before a van will pick us up to take us to dinner, so we toss our bags on the bed and arrange our clothes for a four-day stay. Suddenly, the low buzz of outdoor activity is pierced by the call to evening prayer. Dozens of minarets - slender spires stretching into the sky - broadcast the sacred chants from loudspeakers mounted high on their sides, filling the air with solemn intonements to join in prayer to Allah. Moving like the gentle winds that carry them through the night, the voices wrap themselves around and throughout the city, reminding us that Istanbul has a rich spiritual identity that balances the modern business juggernaut that makes it such an appealing force in the region.

The call is jarring when it first breaks across our ears, but in time, it will become like the pleasant singing voice of a friend whose arrival we instinctively anticipate at specific times of the day. It is only the late-night call that disturbs our slumber each evening that momentarily upsets us, before we roll in our beds to return to sleep.

But tonight, on our first evening in the city, Mesut has arranged for us to eat at Fenners Fish Restaurant - a small but popular café whose tables spill down the front steps and onto the sidewalk. The air is nippy, but the wine warms us as we order our meals and street musicians position themselves around us. Once we tip them, they move into the café. Rolls and more wine satisfy us as we wait for our appetizers and main courses (a combination of shrimp, scallops, and salmon that fill my stomach quite nicely, thank you). The night breeze is now barely noticed, as dessert finds its way to our table.

As we arrive back in our hotel, the day's final call to prayer reverberates about the city.

4.

Having a personal guide to the city is a new experience for us. While cognizant of the main attractions that tourists want to see, a personal guide can tailor her presentation to the one or two individuals that she has under her watch. Our ages, our personalities, and our interests and rudimentary knowledge of Istanbul figure into her routine, as does her quick assessment of our physical conditions; her stride and her patter of information is gauged to our own pace and understanding. And she can pivot, as the need arrives, to display knowledge and locations based on our own requests as the day progresses. It also helps that, in our case, our guide's uncle runs one of the best eateries in the Old Town.

Just before 9 A.M., Güzin arrives at our hotel. She is an attractive woman in her mid-forties, dressed casually but professionally for an all-day walk through the city south of the Golden Horn. We have a steep uphill walk to get to the heart of the Sultanahmet and Faith districts. After winding our way up narrow streets in a confusing maze, we reach a plateau and enter a large series of open squares and plazas. Obelisks taken over years of conquest stand along a stretch of plaza lined by small cobblestoned roads that double as pedestrian walkways filled with tourists and residents.

And to our right, and stretching to a promontory overlooking the junction of the Bosporus and the Golden Horn, are the three most-visited jewels in the city: the Blue Mosque, Hagia Sophia, and Topkapi Palace.

5.

Hiring a personal guide means gaining access to various sites without waiting in the usual admission lines. But even with this advantage, Güzin notes that the Blue Mosque is unusually crowded at this early hour. She opts to take us to the Hagia Sophia, then backtrack to what was to have been our first stop. It is a fortuitous choice: the Hagia Sophia is the oldest of the sites that we will visit today.

The Eastern Roman Empire, separated from the Western Roman Empire when it fell in 478 CE, went on to last another thousand years. Today we refer to it as the Byzantine Empire; but make no mistake, its citizens fiercely proclaimed themselves as Romans. In 537 CE, Emperor Justinian I ordered the construction of the largest Greek Orthodox Christian cathedral in what then was the center of Constantinople. It remained the center of the Greek Orthodox patriarchy until 1453 CE, when Sultan Mehmed II and his Ottoman Turks overran the city. The cathedral became a mosque, and the city became the capital of the Ottoman Empire.

In 1932 CE, a decade after the collapse of the Ottomans, Hagia Sophia was designated a museum, and both its Muslim and Christian features and heritages are now on prominent display. Dwarfed by the main entrance, we enter slowly and respectfully.

The first thing we notice is the vastness of the structure's interior. A high-ceiling foyer runs the length of the entrance side, and directly before us is a set of massive wooden doors opened to the nave. Legend has it that the doors are made from the planks of Noah's ark; but, ever the movie buff, I immediately think of the gigantic doors of the wall on Skull Island in *King Kong*. One person's legend….

There are undoubtedly domed mosques and churches larger than the Hagia Sophia in today's world, but a millennium ago, this building held the world record. Standing here today, I can easily believe it. Part construction, part illusion, the interior looks staggering in its height. Marred only by a section of scaffolding on one side (and *that* being a light, unobtrusive grey), the inside of this church turned mosque turned museum conveys the awesome power and grandeur that its builders intended. It is a curious dance we all perform, as the multitude of visitors drift through the open stretch of floor alternately looking up and then following structural lines down to the floor - all without major collisions between groups.

The second level, high above the crowded first floor, forms a wide balcony, allowing for views of the entire nave from top to bottom. Getting to that balcony is a daunting feat: inclined passageways, with only the occasional step, weave back and forth until, finally, the path opens upon a level surface. By then, my legs are screaming - and the rest of my body is none too happy either. Words cough out sporadically until our breathing regulates itself again. Güzin merely smiles; she has made this climb so many times that she has to slow down as we struggle to reach the top.

6.

Hagia Sophia had, in one form or another, stood in the Old Town for almost a millennium before the arrival of the Ottoman Turks. During that time, the entire town occupied the peninsula of what today is the southern half of the European side of Istanbul. Its northern boundary, then, was the Golden Horn, a curved estuary branching off of the Bosporus.

Over the centuries, the Byzantine Empire fell only once, for almost sixty years. In 1204, the Fourth Crusade went rogue, was excommunicated by the Pope, and sacked and occupied Constantinople instead of heading for the Holy Land. Reconquered by the Romans in 1261, the internal damage to the Byzantine lands caused a gradual decline in the restored empire. By the mid-1450s, Constantinople *was* the empire.

The Golden Horn had remained the city's salvation. Able to repel land attacks, the city had extended a massive chain across the mouth of the river, keeping foreign fleets at bay and the northern shore defended. Until 1453 - when Mehmed II decided to simply go around the chain. His sailors hauled their ships over the mountains of the northern peninsula, and the Romans awoke to the sight of a Persian fleet parked at their doorstep. Constantinople, and the Empire, fell swiftly. The Ottoman Empire had a new capital.

On the Hagia Sophia's second level, Connie and I gaze, not just at Muslim artwork and architecture, but at restored fragments of Christian art. Under Persian control, the cathedral became a mosque, and frescoes of Jesus and his followers were considered blasphemous.

Strictly interpreted, Islam considers any representation of prophets or saints to be a violation of the Jewish bible's second commandment against idols. Earlier artworks along the mosque's walls were covered over and replaced by the geometric stylings of Muslim artists.

Only in the past century have the Christian artworks been restored, partially destroyed by the overlay of later works. We can still see the colorful, if somewhat muted, images of Jesus, Mary, and a host of other disciples and saints. These walls seem almost bright compared to the shadowed interior of the nave. Somehow the midday sun fails to fully illuminate the Hagia Sophia's interior; but it does little to diminish the grandeur of this beautiful structure.

We descend to the first floor the same way that we came up. One last look into the nave, and we exit into the growing heat of the day.

7.

Across the impeccably trimmed lawns and the narrow street that separate it from the Hagia Sophia, the Blue Mosque stands bleached by the midday sun. The crowds have thinned out, and Güzin leads us into a large courtyard where, before entering the mosque, we must remove our shoes. Men may wear headgear, and so my porkpie hat passes muster as we head to the entrance; women must cover their heads, so Connie is given a light grey shawl that she anchors by wrapping one end around her neck.

I am nothing if not opportunistic. The camera is up at my eyes by the time Connie's head and shoulders are draped, and she instinctively smiles at me for an instant. It is all the time I need. The camera clicks repeatedly, before her smile fades. I have my prize: a choice piece of blackmail - her grown son would be so upset - that will share space with baby pictures of my daughter that I can show to her fiancé (whenever she gets one) and photos of my card-playing buddies from our drunken evenings around the table.

As we enter the mosque, I am once again amazed at the utilization of design techniques that create such a vast and powerful interior. No extraneous materials and no excess furnishings mar the clean, bright, and colorful expanse of either the outer passageways or of the prayer area that they ring. The massive interior buzzes with a respectful collection of murmurs as visitors are funneled along lush rugs and kept discreetly away from the carpets being used by the faithful at prayer.

Because it is a functioning place of worship, access to areas within the Blue Mosque is strictly limited. Our time, therefore, passes quickly; within the hour, we are putting our shoes on and heading for a meal.

8.

Just a block away from the Hagia Sophia, our guide's uncle runs the Lale Restaurant, also known as The Pudding Shop (for its renowned custard creations). The sun is baking the pavement, and shade persists in clinging to the opposite side of the street; we head inside to an empty table in a corner nook.

Food is displayed, in lieu of an outdoor menu, under slanted glass, tempting customers as they decide what to consume. The glass-topped offerings sit on either side of the entrance as we pass into the eatery, and continue along one side of the interior as we sit. My choice is simple and obvious: salmon and rice. Thankfully, the gods have favored the establishment with incredibly gifted chefs, and my meal - familiar as it is - is the best I've tasted in weeks. A glass of rosé wine complements the fish, and all is suddenly cool and comfortable in this tiny pocket of my life.

The restaurant buzzes with conversation and activity; it seems as if everybody knows everyone in the place. Soon the banter extends to us, first to Güzin as a known regular, and then to Connie and I. I love the people here - open, friendly, and curious, without the hint of resentment toward Americans that we pick up elsewhere in Europe. We talk about the food first, and then, feeling more secure and accepted, other topics open for discussion - nothing too heavy, and definitely not politics. We're all indulging our appetites and thirsts, and hiding from the rising heat of the afternoon.

Of course, it has to end. The clientele has to vacate the tables for the next influx of customers; the maneuver is done with the practiced grace of years of experience. We follow Güzin's lead as we press our way to the street. We don't know it yet, but we are on our way to a magic carpet ride in the heart of the city.

9.

Güzin is telling us something about Mehmed II, but a full stomach and the incredibly oppressive heat of the early afternoon is playing havoc with my body and my mind. Confusion and wobbly legs are a nasty combination, and I fight to hide the effects as we turn into a side street. Blessedly, Güzin guides us into a small building in a narrow, nondescript passage in the center of the southern business district. As with most guided tours, our day will include a stop at a local merchant who will try to sell us some of his goods. We accept this as a routine practice for Güzin, and, having developed an easy friendship over the morning hours, we trust her to bring us to a reputable seller.

Carpets, of course, are Turkey's most notable product, and the weavers in these establishments are rightly proud of their creations. After a brief tour of the work areas, Connie is instructed in, and given the chance to attempt, the art of weaving a small part of a carpet. She does quite well, while I sit and knock back a drink and supervise.

Now the sales pitch begins in earnest. As in Ephesus, the display of carpets is magnificently choreographed. The kaleidoscope of colors and patterns is dizzying and yet, at the same time, distinct and compelling - so much so that we leave the building as the proud owners of two large rugs and a rather small, framed carpet miniature that Connie has fallen in love with.

But if we think our spending for the day has ended....

10.

Refreshed by the natural coolness of the building that we just left - and the cold drinks that were generously offered - we are briskly led down another narrow, busy street to Istanbul's Grand Bazaar. Even in retrospect, so many months later, I am still dumbfounded by this...money-sucking, awesomely magnificent, heart-stoppingly amazing collection of the most eclectic shops gathered under one series of arched roofs. And even that description is woefully inadequate to describe not just the sights of the market, but the senses and sensations stirred by a short afternoon in this product wonderland.

The Bazaar dates back to 1455, just after Mehmed II's conquest of the city. It grew over the centuries to its current size during the rule of the Ottoman sultans, and the complex now includes cafés, fountains, and even a mosque; the passageways are continuously clogged by shoppers vying for the best deals at over 4,000 storefronts. The urge to resist modernization has left the marketplace with that fascinating mix of familiar (western) and alien (eastern).

This may well be the first time that I have gotten lost in a large area that is set up on a strict grid system. Impossible, you say? I would have agreed with you before entering the Bazaar. But I am here now, and the only thing holding my directional sanity together is the presence of Güzin, who navigates the market as if she had laid it out herself. And even she is surprised as we find stores that have items that I'm looking for that she had no interest in. This monstrously large bazaar is literally a grid of up-and-down and side-by-side passages that house dozens of shops in large defined squares, and yet…Connie and I are more disoriented than we've ever been.

But that does not stop our pillaging of storefronts, grabbing and paying for shirts, bags, figurines of Greek soldiers (yes, Greek - if it brings in cash, the merchants will stock it), souvenir magnets, and whatever else strikes our avaricious fancy before we leave the market with our hands and bags full.

This is your one-stop Ugly American shopping spot! And we *will* return before we leave the city!

11.

Stretching along the Seraglio Point, a promontory that towers over the junction of the Golden Horn and the Bosporus, is Topkapi Palace. Commissioned by Constantinople's conquerer, Mehmed II, it is comprised of four courtyards, each entered consecutively. And although the palace has been expanded over the centuries - to complement the expansion of the Ottoman Empire - the basic layout has remained the same.

Eventually, the sultans built other palaces along the banks of the Bosporus (enabling merchants and other workers to build up the northern side of the Golden Horn). Topkapi Palace was used only occasionally then, and after the Ottomans fell out of power in the early 20th century, it was turned into a museum.

An entire day could easily be spent at Topkapi Palace. But it is mid-afternoon, and we must utilize every moment of sunlight remaining. That means, for me, that I must photograph building interiors first, using the ambient light available; then, as the sun sinks below the Golden Horn and bathes everything in a vibrant orange hue, I must quickly train my camera on the building exteriors and the spacious green lawns that fill each courtyard.

We reach the palace's main entry point. Each courtyard opens to elaborately detailed structures that house some of the most dazzling displays of weaponry, period clothing, relics and artifacts from Christian and Muslim history, along with diligently-written manuscripts and documents. Photographing these items is largely forbidden, although I see no shortage of tourists surreptitiously taking shots with their smartphones. The smattering of guards strolling through the rooms is unequal to the task of fully enforcing any ban.

Güzin does her best to get us as much time as possible, but the palace design is like a Russian nesting egg: each courtyard leads to another more spectacular setting. The sheer size of the palace ensures that we will have to return - if not this trip, then at some future date. But before we must retrace our steps through all four courtyards, I get one final treat. At the far end of the grounds, I can photograph the European side of Istanbul from atop the promontory; and pivoting on my heel, I can turn and shoot the Asian side of the city - a brilliant panoramic image of a town that has become my favorite stop on this voyage.

12.

Istanbul lies at our feet the following morning as we head to the upper level of the Hop-on Hop-off bus that will introduce us to the urban landscape of the city. After rumbling through the streets below the Golden Horn, we head up a highway that parallels the water; a quick right turn takes us across the Horn to the northern European side.

The difference is not as cathartic as we thought it would be. Yes, some of the streets are wider, with storefronts and buildings showing a more modern look to the city. But the architecture quickly becomes a mix of the upscale and of the crowded older shops with hundreds of people milling about. It softens the culture shock that we were anticipating; the transition to modern is relaxed, inevitable.

And then we see the line of stores along a wide stretch of boulevard: MacDonalds, Starbucks, Burger

King, and KFC. The transition is complete; ahead lie monolithic business structures and apartment buildings. Istanbul has perfected the blending of old and new, of traditional and modern. The bus' recorded message rambles on in our earplugs, but we largely ignore it. This is a living city, and it has its own vibrant cacophony of sights and voices and background noise; it assaults the senses, and heightens the feeling of excitement running through us.

Then we are crossing the Bosporus. As we reach the other side, a yellow sign with black letters says, "Welcome to Asia." Well…I've never been welcomed by an entire continent before! I've had some customs guards welcome me half-heartedly to their countries; I've had head waiters welcome me wholeheartedly to their restaurants. But an entire continent? I am impressed, to say the least. I wonder if I should have at least brought a bottle of wine for my hosts. But then we suddenly turn around and return over the bridge. He doesn't say anything, but there is a definitely implied, "OK, now you've been there; cross it off your list," from the bus driver. We cross the river.

Europe doesn't welcome us.

13.

I always thought that Paris' sanisettes were Europe's low point when it comes to public restrooms. I was so wrong. Some of Istanbul's duty accommodations require users to engage in physical acrobatics that are truly Olympian: decathlon meets the hokey-pokey.

I discover this reality one afternoon during an emergency stop along the southern bank of the Golden Horn. Even though somewhat prepared by photos and warnings in guide books, the actual confrontation with this minimalist version of a rest stop is jaw-dropping. I enter and close a metal door behind me, and I freeze as I face a barren, blue-tiled cubicle.

There is no toilet as I know it: no bowl, no seat, no…anything. Well, that's not entirely true. Despite the proliferation of small, square blue tiles covering the walls, ceiling, and floor, there is a large, porcelain indentation in the floor before me - as if a 20-foot tall human had parked his butt on the cold tiles and left a gleaming white imprint (complete with a large hole). And - lucky for me - he left a roll of tissue paper along the left wall.

My mind, after it lets out a hideous scream, empties and begins working on a plan. I drop my trousers and squat as much as a man who doesn't include squats in his daily exercise routine can. Realizing that I can only hold this position for a few seconds, my left hand reaches to the left wall and presses in. Still a bit wobbly; so my right hand finds the tiles on the right wall, and now I'm pushing on either side and suspending myself over the porcelain imprint. I'm Doolittle sighting my target as I buzz Tokyo; I look like a spider, splayed across the cubicle.

Moments later, my mission is accomplished, and my brain is working out the logistics of reaching the tissue paper in front of my left foot. My right foot shoots out toward the wall, and lodges where it meets the floor; pressure is applied, and my right hand is free. If there is a God above, the next move should assure me of a position on any Olympic gymnastic team in the world: I swing my straightened right arm out and down diagonally across my body as I bend forward and sweep the tissue roll up to my neck. There, securing the roll between my chest and my chin, I use my right hand alone to secure a sufficient amount of paper to accomplish my next task. I repeat the move as often as needed. I drop the roll, pull myself to a standing position, and fix my appearance. My arms and legs are screaming at me. I mutter something to myself about an emergency, but my limbs are having none of it.

Connie tells me that I've been "in there" a while. I look at her and bite my tongue. Then, as I start to walk, she asks me what is wrong with me. "My arms and legs hurt." She gives me a quizzical look, then shakes her head. I shrug my shoulders.

My shoulders hurt now.

14.

A burial ground would seem an odd spot to find a delightful little café, and yet here, at the top of the Eyüp Cemetery, sits just such an establishment. Odder still, it is named for the French novelist and travel writer who frequented the café during his stays in Istanbul (then Constantinople), and it has become a major tourist spot on the outskirts of town. Pierre Loti was the naval officer-turned-writer who "discovered" this perch high above Istanbul, and who, in effect, spearheaded the tourist surge that brings much-needed money into the neighborhood.

That income is helpful compensation for an area that has seen better days: the Ottoman elite established the neighborhood and the cemetery, and Muslims had made the hill a place of pilgrimage in previous centuries; now tourism fills the gap, as buses unload foreign visitors anxious to see the views from observation stands around the café.

Mesut has arranged a bus-and-boat tour of the city and surroundings for us; we have to hustle, as the bus will arrive at the hotel at 9 A.M. promptly. Once aboard, we are heading in the opposite direction from the Sultanahmet district across southern Istanbul. Our destination, arrived at via a tortuous passage by our tour vehicle through narrow streets and hairpin turns around corner shops, is one of the highest points in the city on the European side: Eyüp Cemetery. Our guide gives us ten minutes to explore the area, and then we are to meet him on the paved observation decks.

Below the decks, a pair of small cable cars wait to transport us to the bottom of the hill, where our bus awaits. The views on the descent are striking, as the still-clinging morning haze rises to reveal more of the Golden Horn and its northeastern shore - we have almost reached the "tip" of the Horn, and the northern shore is curving into its eastern border. The bus rumbles around the base of the hill, revealing elaborate mausoleums and tombs for the deceased elite; above them, we see the section of graves reserved for public executioners from the Ottoman period, and then the cemetery climbs up into the dissipating mist.

Our return to the center of Istanbul takes us through the enormous stone arches that are the last prominent reminders of empire: the Valens Aquaduct. Barely wide enough for a bus or car to slip through, traffic nonetheless whips through the narrow arches with frightening speed and accuracy. Other ancient structures, north of the Golden Horn, have long since been demolished in the name of progress and expansion. Crossing the Horn, we drive through the widening boulevards and slip between the towering monoliths of northern European Istanbul.

15.

Twenty minutes in the northern half of European Istanbul make us nostalgic for the hours that we spent exploring the Blue Mosque, the Grand Bazaar, and any number of other wonders south of the Golden Horn. Modernized in the 17th and 18th centuries, ancient city walls were destroyed to provide room for apartments and commercial properties, spurred on by the sultans' abandonment of the Topkapi Palace for the development of residences along the Bosporus shore. Chief among these is the Dolmabahçe Palace.

Built in the 1850s, Dolmabahçe Palace was conceived as the summer residence for the sultan, but upon its completion, it also served as government administrative offices. It is now a museum, with most of its architectural features and interior furnishings preserved for tourists. And after an hour of driving past commercial skyscrapers and neighborhood Starbucks, another hour in this national treasure is sweet relief for us as we tumble from our bus.

Much like Topkapi, we must pass through multiple gateways and courtyards; but the spaces here are compressed, and we are standing in the entrance of the palace within minutes. The building is an enormous, multi-floored rectangle. Plush carpets hemmed by velvet ropes lead us through a well-thought-out pathway that takes us from one end of the structure to the other, navigating stairs with an efficiency that prevents boondoggles with other groups of visitors.

The various rooms, some expansive and some surprisingly intimate, are stunningly appointed - and without that oppressive stench of age that older furniture usually carries. Artwork from various centuries is hung or - in the case of statuaries - pedestalled throughout the tour route; and despite the ban on taking photographs in certain areas, the easily-recognized clicks of smartphone cameras reverberate through the halls.

We exit on the east side of the palace, and from an elevated terrace, we see that we are just a few yards from the Bosporus. One of several ornate, arched metal gates leading to a concrete boat landing is directly opposite us. Cameras click wildly; being this close to the water, with such a fantastic view, is a rarity in this town that excites all of the picture-takers among us.

Our guide gathers us; the bus driver's part of our tour is ending, and he is anxious to deposit us at the wharf and to call it a day.

16.

Water laps against the wharf as we wait for our boat to arrive. Blown in from the Bosporus, the wind sends a chill down our backs; without jackets, we realize too late that the afternoon sun will not protect us from the strong breezes whipping above the waves.

If boats are like people, then the craft that arrives to gather us up is a slightly-decrepit middle-aged man. Wheezing at the dock, it takes us aboard; the residual waves from other vessels plowing through the strait reach the wharf and gently rock our boat just enough to make us hesitate as we calculate the slight jump we must execute to get aboard. Once on deck, we proceed into the lower cabin.

The weathered vessel has two decks: an enclosed dining room with a small buffet set up in the rear; and an open upper deck with a canvas topping held taut by metal rods reaching up from the wooden rails. We take our seats as the boat pulls away from land and starts a circuit that will include a tour of the Golden Horn followed by a cruise up the Bosporus almost to the Black Sea. There, the waters of other sovereign states will force us down along the Asian side of the Strait and back to Istanbul.

We order drinks, then march to the rear to be confronted by the Mother of All Lousy Buffets. "Anemic" would be high praise for this collection of poorly cooked chicken, seafood(?), and vegetables. It is going to be a long, hungry afternoon. We order more drinks.

As we leave the Horn behind, I climb to the top deck, camera in hand. We pass the Dolmabahçe Palace on our left, giving me a unique opportunity to digitally capture the structure from offshore and complement my previous shots from the morning. Farther along the waterline, extending inland and uphill are the remains of the city fortifications from centuries past.

But my initial excitement is blown away by the cold blasts of air being funneled along the top of the boat. The combination of canvas overhead sheeting and the rods and railings is forcing gusts of wind directly through the second deck; the effect seems magnified with each new breeze. I finally give up, and retreat to the lower cabin.

An hour later, returning south, the boat docks at a small town on the Asian shore miles above Istanbul. We are allowed to go ashore and spend a half-hour walking through the village. We stay mostly along the extended waterfront; the shops, from long experience, have positioned themselves along this stretch as souvenir merchants, and their owners stand in doorways with pleasant greetings extended to all of us - but especially to those willing to delve further into the stores and shop.

Back at the boat, we are again calculating distances, wind factors, and other variables as the prow of our boat bobs up and down against the wharf. A young seaman from the boat aids Connie in navigating the step-over. I watch and think, "hell, no - I'm not going to be meekly guided like an old man" (conveniently forgetting that I'm

69). And as he turns back to help me, I leap - well, I kind of jump - and land on deck upright and with my dignity intact. He looks at me, then gives me a huge grin. I signal him back with a thumbs-up, and we both laugh.

As I head for the cabin, my ankles, my knees, and my brain all scream at me: "Ow ow ow! Are you insane? Don't ever do that again!"

17.

A final afternoon in Istanbul calls for a walk along the southern shore of the Golden Horn. Earlier, we rode past the hotel where Agatha Christie reputedly wrote <u>Murder on the Orient Express</u>; now we are walking past the old and neglected block-long facade of the Istanbul train station - where, once upon a time, passengers would enter to board the Orient Express and other fabled rail lines.

Farther along, we see the entrance to the Spice Bazaar, an L-shaped marvel of sights, sounds, and, especially, smells. Outwardly resembling a narrow factory, the orange-tan building extends along one side of a crowded plaza separated from the water by a multi-lane boulevard. At the corner of the square, the Bazaar makes a sharp left turn away from it. This shorter line of the building empties into the bustling streets of the market area.

But inside the structure.... Like the Grand Bazaar, the roof is a series of arches and domes; they seem higher because the hallway is not as packed with shops seemingly tumbling over themselves, and the lighter-colored ceiling seems to reflect the ambient light back onto the crowded passageway. Some storefronts hawk clothes and other trinkets, but the majority of the shops have plexiglass mini-stalls that display a rainbow array of crushed and powdered spices. The effect is almost psychedelic. The scents flowing through the two hallways are lush and full; curiosity overcomes our senses, and both Connie and I are drawn to explore what these spices are and how they season the foods we eat.

Something breaks the spell. The siren call of the Grand Bazaar in the late afternoon pulls at us and our wallets. We find - with some difficulty - one of the entrances, and we lose ourselves to the grid-maze that is the Bazaar. Wending our way through the hallways, we discover crafts, statuettes, pipes, and a cornucopia of tourist delights…and we spend. Oh, we spend - shamelessly, hopelessly, almost hypnotically.

A voice shouts in my head. "Get out!" It's a buzzing at first, like an annoying mosquito; within seconds, it is pounding through my brain. "GET OUT!" Well, if you insis…."GET OUT!"

We find our way to the hotel.

18.

I'm not a cruel person by nature. But every once in a great while, I like to shock someone (in a harmless way) to see their reaction. The statement I make one afternoon in Istanbul's Grand Bazaar is intended to get a rise out of Connie; but the effect it has on a pair of merchants is more priceless than I could have ever anticipated.

I used to smoke a pipe religiously. Over the past few decades, I've cut back to a few times a year. But I still have a spot in my heart for meerschaum pipes: the virgin whiteness of the bowl when it's new, replaced over time and use by the brown and black discoloration that gives the pipe it's distinctive final look. And now, standing in the Grand Bazaar, I have a feast of new meerschaums to peruse in a small corner shop.

These shops - really little more than stalls stuffed with product - allow enough room for two customers and two merchants. A middle-aged man, thin with sharp eyes and a pencil mustache, runs the pipe shop with a young lady (wife? sister?) who sits behind a cash register. The man is showing me pipes.

As I consider the various shapes and sizes of meerschaums, he asks an innocent question, "Are you getting this for display, or for smoking?" In the same breath, Connie says "display" while I blurt out "smoking." I look over at my wife with a grin as she gasps, "*smoking?*"

"Well," I say, "I've got cancer; what more harm can it do?"

The proverbial pin could have dropped. And as I look beyond Connie, I see sheer horror on the cashier's face. "Oh my God, he's said the quiet part out loud." It seems an eternity before she turns her head down and starts fumbling with her hands.

The man says nothing. His somewhat robotic movements tell me that he is struggling with a response that never comes. Surprised by the trifecta of reactions, I give everyone a chance to breathe and collect themselves. I choose a pipe.

Outside, Connie playfully chides me. "Bad Wes, bad Wes."

Yes…yes, I am.

19.

For almost two millennia, Istanbul has served

as the capital for a succession of empires: the last of the prominent Greek city-states and the most easterly; the Eastern Roman Empire and its Byzantine successor; and the Ottoman Empire, spanning, at one time, Asia Minor and Mesopotamia to the east, and eastern Europe to the outskirts of Vienna in the west. And then it ended.

Not all at once, of course. By the middle of the 18th century, Ottoman attempts to modify their society to bring it more in line with western European progress only stirred nationalist feelings that would weaken the central government. In the early 20th century, the Balkan Wars damaged the western side of the Empire.

But it was the Empire's decision to align itself with the Central Powers (Germany and Austro-Hungary) during World War I that sealed its doom. Defeated and occupied by the Allies in 1918, it was the nationalist movement under Mustafa Kemel Pasha (later, Kemel Ataturk) that would drive foreign forces from Turkey and abolish the Ottoman Sultanate in 1922.

In 1923, the Republic of Turkey was formally recognized. Ankara became the country's capital, to disassociate the new nation from the memory of empire.

But Istanbul remains the country's most popular city for travelers and historians.

20.

Late in the afternoon, alone and on the third day of our stay in Istanbul, we struggle to find our way from the Blue Mosque to our hotel. I know that we have to move downhill toward the Bosporus; I know the road we have to start on to reach our destination; I have days of experience and map-reading to ensure that we find our way. And we are lost.

Twenty minutes separate the Blue Mosque from the Antea Palace Hotel. We have been winding along streets and alleys for two hours. The area is not vast - it's remarkably compressed, in fact. But we keep coming around to other parts of Sultanahmet. The roads in this area are like the threads of a large ball that has come undone and wend a serpentine path around the peninsula.

I cannot begin to fathom the mind of the architect of this system of broad streets, narrow lanes, and cobblestoned paths that alternately pass through older residential neighborhoods and stretches of small shops. In some areas, the slightly-more-than one lane passages are hemmed in by minuscule raised sidewalks; and despite the width of the roads, they are open to traffic in both directions. People lean out of their houses or shops to check on sidewalk traffic, and Connie and I become a part of a treacherous game of doorway hopping. Pedestrians walk along the one-person-wide sidewalks, vigilantly checking for two-way car traffic - for when cars pass each other along these narrow lanes, one vehicle must jump a curb and ride a sidewalk during the actual passing. Our survival depends on being near, or finding, a recessed doorway and leaping into it as cars whisk past us, brushing our pants.

After almost two hours of this vigorous activity, we are worn, hungry, and frustrated. But, for all that, I am thrilled, as the city opens itself before me. For this is the essence of travel for me - to lose myself in a loud, colorful, historically packed city, not knowing what cultural, culinary, or architectural wonders I might stumble upon at any moment.

And Istanbul is all of that. When we leave, I know that I will return. I will find more secrets, more little passages to explore. Because that can be the best part about traveling in a new or favorite city: getting lost.

AACHEN

1.

What to make of the Holy Roman Empire? Voltaire described it as "neither holy, nor Roman, nor an empire," and he was correct - at least during the first few centuries of its existence. Only after the 13th century did its true form become clear, when it was first referred to in writings by its full name: the Holy Roman Empire of the German Nation. From its beginnings as a papal military arm to its final manifestation as a German kingdom (the First Reich), the "empire" spanned a thousand years.

Established in 800 CE, its roots went back 400 years to the fall of the Western Roman Empire. With no Roman emperor, and overrun by barbarians who had embraced the new Christian faith, the pope decided to fill the leadership vacuum. He took up the reins of his empire of souls and moved to strengthen the church's continued survival in the secular world. Around the same time, the Frankish tribes took over the former Roman territories in northern Gaul - present-day France and Germany.

Frankish tribes were united by Clovis, one of their warriors who had converted to Christianity. One of his successors, Pepin the Short - did the Franks really refer to their kings by the names have come down to us such as Charles the Bald, Louis the Pious, and Charles the Fat? - expanded the Frankish lands to include present-day Switzerland, Austria, and Hungary. Pepin's empire was coming dangerously close to Italy's Papal States.

Pope Leo III moved decisively to offset the danger. On Christmas Day in 800 CE, in Rome,, he crowned Pepin's son, Charlemagne, as King of the Romans - in effect, the first Holy Roman Emperor, responsible for the protection of the Catholic Church in Europe. By then, Charlemagne had secured the northern Italian provinces for the pope, although they remained Germanic possessions.

And what has this to do with Aachen, Germany? Charlemagne was crowned as German king in this city. For the next 500 years, the vast majority of German monarchs, starting with Charlemagne's son Louis, were crowned in Aachen before being proclaimed Holy Roman

Emperor in Rome. Although never officially named as such, half a millennium's coronations, plus Charlemagne's establishment of his court there, warrant a view of the city as the empire's first capital.

2.

The choice of Aachen as a part of our itinerary may seem odd, especially given the selection of other cities that comprise our travel plans - Rome, Athens, Istanbul, and, later, Vienna. But beyond the *historical* connection with Charlemagne and empire, Aachen holds a *personal* connection for my family and I.

In 1944, Aachen was the first German city that my father entered as an infantryman during World War II. As he and two other soldiers swept a street for signs of enemy action, a German soldier opened fire on them with a machine-gun, taking all three men down. As the first shots rang out, my father pivoted, and a bullet hit him in the chest. Waking later in the hospital, he realized what had happened: the thick, pocket-sized bible that the Army had issued to each soldier, and that my father carried in his shirt pocket, had taken the main force of the chest shot, and the bullet had only barely broken the skin's surface.

As kids, we heard that story so many times that we could recite it in our heads as Dad regaled us with the tale once more. It became a part of our family history. And now, my wife and I are heading into Aachen, rebuilt from the massive damage that it had suffered during the war.

Oh, and my father - he received a Purple Heart, prepared to go home, and was shipped back to the front lines...where he was wounded again, received his second Purple Heart, prepared to be sent home, and was transported to the front again. Like it or not, he was in this war for keeps.

3.

I am a bit edgy as we hurtle through the countryside in a high-speed train. Although I view most forms of transportation as just a means to get from one spot to another, there is something about rail travel - trains, trams, and trolleys - that appeals to the romantic traveler in me. But the TGV cars glide so smoothly along the tracks that the familiar clickity-clack of wheels against steel is missing, and without it, somehow, some of the thrill of the journey.

Still, there is, outside the car, the swift passage of land as trees, hedges, and villages whiz by - a sensation that is missing in an airplane that, paradoxically enough, screams through the air at much faster speeds. Clouds just hang in place as a craft cuts through the sky, generating a sense of...nothing. No, thank you, I'll take a train if given the choice.

And so we are barreling toward Aachen, and I'm not sure what to expect there. The war devastated the city; rebuilt, it is undoubtably different from the town that my father knew. But I also know that, at its heart, there remains the cathedral that held the coronation of Charlemagne and of his son, along with 500 years worth of monarchs who were crowned "King of the Germans" beneath its dome - before they became Holy Roman

Emperors.

The train glides to a halt; we disembark and leave the station, entering a wide plaza opening onto the city. Taxis wait to one side, and soon we are ripping through town, past quaint cobblestoned streets and - in short order - a more modern set of roads passing an enclosed mall. The route seems circular rather than direct - necessary, or an extravagance of the driver? No matter. Before we can question him, we are in front of our hotel: the Aquis Grana. Scalloped sides to the hotel allow every room to have a clear view of the Aachen Cathedral just a few blocks away. As the hour is late, we choose a small café to grab a sandwich and a beer, and retire.

4.

Most large European cities share a common historical point of reference: they progress from small villages to Roman outposts, usually trading centers. Aachen, by contrast, was used by Roman soldiers along the frontier to relax and unwind from the stress of border duty by indulging in the hot-water springs that flowed from mountain vents. Aachen, or Aix-la Chapelle (as it was also known), was a spa town - still is, for that matter.

The city was chosen by Charlemagne as his seat of power for its pivotal location in his united Frankish kingdom. Its ongoing popularity springs as much from its historical importance to the forming German nation as to the continued attraction of its spas.

5.

Our breath is visible as we walk through the chill of the morning air. Here in the northwestern corner of Germany, late October is reminding us that winter - and the end of our trip - is fast approaching.

A short walk takes us to the south face of the Aachen Cathedral, which looms above us with its multitude of statues gazing out over the city. It's as if every saint known to man (or priest) has scaled the sides of the church and found a niche in which to pose. The cathedral itself, with its adjoining buildings, displays three distinct architectural styles, reflecting the ongoing process of building and adding on structures over the centuries.

Charlemagne's original building, the Palatine Chapel, is an octagonal monument built in the Carolingian-Romanesque style, as it was completed during the first emperor's reign. Ottonian and Gothic flourishes completed the church structures. Although badly damaged during World War II, the cathedral was completely restored.

This is my Holy Grail in Germany: the resting place of Charlemagne himself, and the crude stone throne that looks down upon it from its second-floor perch. Charlemagne's coronation as "King of the Germans" in Aachen Cathedral, and his subsequent investiture as "King of the Romans," would ensure the place of Christianity as western civilizations's preeminent religion; and the kingdoms that his rule united would form the foundations of Europe's great nations (France, Germany, and Austria, among others). History pivots in this cathedral.

Connie and I head to the west side of the church, where our guided tour will begin. In perfect, clipped

English, a university student walks us through the stained-glass and candle-lit interior, stopping under the huge dome for effect. Then we proceed to a gated nave that contains - among other treasures - the solid-gold ossuary holding the remains of Charlemagne. Our guide's words fade into the ether. I am conscious only of being in the presence of greatness: another tomb, another portal through time. This is why I travel.

My wife nudges me. It is her sad duty to always tear me away from greatness and back to the present. We ascend to the church's second level: a wide balcony that rings the first floor beneath the dome. There we see Charlemagne's throne. A remarkably unattractive set of beige stone blocks come together to form a bare-bones seat whose elevation allows its occupant to view the entire lower floor. Our guide is talking again…I think. Connie nudges me.

The tour over, I realize that I have neglected to photograph the golden ossuary. Only members of a tour accompanied by an official guide are allowed to open the gate and enter the nave. But I want my photo - and so I become the Ugly American. To my wife's utter horror ("You *never* break rules!"), I swing the gate wide and try to bluff my way in. To the brusque, solidly-built guard, I argue that I *was* a part of a guided tour, just not the one that is there at present. He doesn't buy it, but now others have passed through the gate that I opened, and he angrily tells me to get my pictures while he herds the other offenders out. Then it's our turn to leave. We exit the cathedral and head toward the north wall, as Connie continues to sputter.

"But you *never* break the rules!"

6.

When Charlemagne dies, his empire is divided amongst his sons into three kingdoms. The western region will eventually become most of present-day France, with a strong central monarchy; the Kingdom of Italy, as you probably expect, will eventually fall to a united Italian nation. The eastern kingdom becomes a collection of duchies and principalities ruled by their own princes and barons. The Holy Roman Emperor holds nominal power, but is essentially an arbiter of judicial matters between the various polities within the empire.

Deprived of its central position of influence, Aachen eventually cedes its position as empire "capital." Frankfurt will claim that position, followed by a number of other claimants. Once the House of Habsburg comes to power, it will move the capital to Vienna - turning that city into a spiritual center as well as the secular capital of Austria-Hungary.

Aachen's appeal remains, nonetheless. Still a spa town, it becomes a beacon for pilgrims who wish to visit the tomb of Charlemagne and to see a fabled collection of other relics that are put on display every seven years; the next scheduled presentation is in 2021 CE.

7.

The Aachen Rathaus (town hall), built around 1330 CE, sits between two squares: south of the hall, a large plaza stretches out to the north side of the cathedral; northward, a smaller cobblestoned area serves multiple functions. Today, it holds a bustling fresh-food market, with vendors and visitors winding past the overflowing stalls in the brisk afternoon air. The vivid odors of oranges, pears, and other fruits and vegetables mingle with the scents of lavender sachets and colorful oddities spilling from boxes and open-doored vans. The resulting maze of aisles meanders across the square in an entertaining slapdash of curiosity, movement, and olfactory delight. Connie and I make a few purchases, and then stroll down side streets lazily wending their way through the older part of town.

As darkness falls, the temperature dips again, but not so much that an outdoor meal is unpleasant. In fact, the night, thick with the smell of tobacco and beer and the laughter of dozens of enthusiastic diners, envelops us with a communal warmth. We have circled our way back to the Rathaus' northern square. The grocery stalls are gone, and tables and chairs have been pulled onto the cobblestones outside of the numerous cafés ringing the plaza. The aroma of steak, seafood, and pasta mix with the heady brew of ales to fill the crisp night air.

We take our time as we enjoy our meals - salmon for me, and glass mugs filled with beer for the both of us. The bitter taste of ale warms our bellies, and the night becomes more soothing, more comforting. We discuss our travel plans for the next day, when we will follow the path of empire to Vienna. And as the evening blurs into a calming buzz, I'm lost in a beer-enhanced reverie as I gaze at Charlemagne's statue watching us from the other side of the square.

8.

Whatever the Holy Roman Empire is, its existence is threatened and then weakened by the Reformation. With so many duchies embracing Protestantism, the empire continually shrinks in size.

Although the Habsburgs rule the Austo-Hungarian Empire from Vienna, their grip on the Holy Roman Empire, tenuous at best, ends - as does the empire itself - in 1806, when Napoleon Bonaparte forces the abdication of the last emperor.

The thousand-year First Reich ends as the German duchies struggle for unity, and empire moves to Paris, briefly, and then to Vienna and to the lands ruled by the Habsburgs.

PARIS

1.

Age cuts strange paths through life for us. Connie and I have visited Paris - alone or together - many times over the years. Connie's experiences have been mixed, at best; but I love the city, and on this, my fourth visit, the overwhelming feeling is one of sadness. I have come to say goodbye to old friends.

Facing an uncertain future, I want to see familiar sites for what may be the last time. And so we set off to visit some old favorites. What I don't expect is that these iconic friends are showing the same signs of advancing age as I am. There is the Eiffel Tower, under a cloudy grey sky, looking worn and discolored - as if in need of a good repainting. Cut off from the rest of the city by glass and metal partitions that allow entry only at the western end of its grounds through security huts and x-ray machines, it is an old man confined to a tightly monitored nursing home.

Connie and I continue to walk along the Seine, past the gardens at the rear of Les Invalides and onward to the green wooden bookstalls lining the road. Here, the bustle of merchants happily selling books, magazines, posters, and other trinkets raises our spirits again. Then we look past the stalls, across the river, and see the missing roof and the burnt-out remains of Notre-Dame Cathedral. The front towers still loom above Île de la Cité; but there is a forlorn look about the whole building that elicits only sorrow.

Turning, I find myself looking at Shakespeare & Co., and for the next hour I am lost in communion with the bookstore. Spirits revived, Connie and I settle into our chairs at the same café where we ate four years earlier when, again, we had indulged our love of books at

Shakespeare's. Slightly different menu, same ambience - and another peaceful hour engulfs us.

Across the street, in a compact park set beside a small church, another old friend awaits: Robinier, Paris' oldest living resident. He is a locust tree, and his roots go back over four hundred years. Age has started to wear on him too; since I last saw him, a new cement brace keeps him upright, along with another beam or two that have been his companions for several years. He is a living witness to Napoleon's reign and to the First French Empire.

2.

With Charlemagne's death, his three sons split his lands. The Western Frankish Empire stabilized much more rapidly than the other two territories (Germany and Italy); a strong central monarchy arose, and these western lands became the country that we know as France. By the late 1780s, the excesses of the monarchs led to the French Revolution, which, in turn, paved the way for an ambitious Corsican soldier to take the reins of power.

Already a national hero by the time that he was 24, Napoleon Bonaparte's rise to power matched his growth in popularity. In 1799, he declared himself First Consul of France (emulating one of his heroes, Julius Caesar); by 1804, Napoleon had declared himself Emperor of the First French Empire. In 1806, he dissolved the Holy Roman Empire - although some think that the last emperor abdicated to prevent Napoleon from declaring himself Holy Roman Emperor. It was of little import - through a series of military engagements and royal intermarriages, Napoleon extended his empire or his influence from Spain to the boundaries of Russia.

And then he pushed too far. His invasion of Russia flew

in the face of both the Russian people's fierce devotion and protection for their nation, and the sheer vastness of the country. The Russian winter did the rest, and as Napoleon retreated, other conquered lands that he had to travel through also revolted. Eventually defeated by an international coalition, Napoleon fell in 1815.

The First French Empire, one of the shortest-lived empires in European history, fell with him. The empire *was* Napoleon - an empire of cult and of personality, and without him it couldn't exist. But he and his reign left a legacy of reform that continues to guide western nations. His Napoleonic Code revolutionized the justice system, and still influences governments to this day.

With Napoleon gone, the monarchy was restored with the Bourbons. Real power, however, moved to the east: the Congress of Vienna resolved the fates of Napoleon's conquered lands; the Habsburgs produced one of their finest rulers in Franz Joseph I; and the joining of Austria and Hungary into one state led to one of the strongest empires that modern Europe would see, ruled, by Franz Joseph, from Vienna.

3.

Our stay in Paris is as short-lived as Napoleon's empire. It is a day's stop as we prepare to fly to Vienna. With luck, we will arrive at our hotel in time to enjoy dinner - and a light white wine.

VIENNA

1.

The empire strikes back, as the House of Habsburg - the last rulers of the Holy Roman Empire - consolidates its power and commands a newly-formed (1867 CE) Austro-Hungarian Empire. With the joining of two powerful nations under one rule, Franz Joseph I will remain the driving force behind a massive domain until his death in 1916.

The new empire will rival the growing - and, in 1870, united - German nation, being a prime mover in the politics of Europe. But it will also become the cultural hub of central Europe, whose turn-of-the-century elegance will profoundly influence music, art, and philosophy. The Ringstrasse - a wide boulevard that encircles the Old Town - not only surrounds the most stunning and important museums, concert halls, and historical buildings; it snares incoming visitors into a world of glistening beauty and impressive architectural wonders.

It is into this most cosmopolitan of European cities that Connie and I fly one evening. Night falls earlier now that October has given way to the shorter autumn hours. As our shuttle whisks us into town, the Danube flows darkly beside us, spattered intermittently by the light of street lamps. We are deposited inside the Ring at its northern end just a few blocks from our hotel.

As the hour is late by the time we get settled in, and the hotel dining room is closed, we walk a block to a small bakery. Apple strudel and hot tea warm me down to my toes, and make for a mild glow at the end of a long day of travel.

2.

Crisp and brisk, Vienna in the morning is a sharp contrast to the languid southern Mediterranean sunrises. Blue skies hemmed by brilliant white clouds hang over the city, while the busy street, swept by a light October breeze, brings the picturesque city into striking focus. Circling the Ringstrasse in the yellow classic tram is tacky and touristy, but is also the best way to get an initial feel for this city that throbs with a fin-de-siècle metropolitan vibe. The complete ride nails down the locations of museums and government buildings for future visits; the majority of iconic structures and cafés sit within the Ring, waiting to be explored.

At the appointed hour, Connie and I join a small group that will be touring the center of town. Our guide - a stout, middle-aged Austrian man of Jewish descent - starts our walk at the Vienna Opera House (which we have already spent an hour circling and photographing) and proceeds along the winding streets and cobblestoned lanes, pointing out landmarks both historical and pop-cultural (several building facades, he notes, have been used as important locations in Hollywood films through the decades).

He also takes us to small monuments and statuaries that honor the Jewish population of Vienna. The city has an ongoing and intertwined relationship with its Jews, not always for the better. Some of the places he takes us are tributes to those who suffered and died (especially during World War II); some of those monuments, sadly, have been defaced by anti-Semitic graffiti - showing a nasty undercurrent of hate that still exists in Vienna.

At the end of the tour, our guide takes his leave, and heads to a nearby café that he says is one of the best in town. He "suggests" that we could probably find it if we happen to follow him as he strolls down the lane. Minutes later, we are seated in the back of Reinthaler's Biest in a crowded hallway - every nook and cranny of this place is utilized by tables, chairs, bars, and stools; loud voices and the aroma of tobacco fill the air, adding to the claustrophobic press of humanity. Somehow we make our desires known, and soon our meals and drinks are placed before us. Our guide has disappeared into the chaos of the back rooms. Time loses meaning here as we eat, drink, and study the human tide swirling around us.

Soon the moment ends, and we push our way back into the street. I have enough of a bearing that I know that we can walk from here to our hotel and to the Metro station one block away. There are places that I must see, and experiences that I must indulge. Two of those await us just a few subway stops north. We head into the Metro.

3.

It is a rare occasion, indeed, when you can stand in front of an entire nation and be informed that, sorry, the country is closed to the public for an indeterminate period of time. Yet here we stand, my wife and I, at a red-and-white-striped wooden door, set into a barbed-wire fence, that says, "Welcome 2 Kugelmugel," and we can go no farther. Kugelmugel is closed.

We are in the Prater, a large city park in the district of the same name. Most of the grounds are occupied by an amusement center that is filled with families out to enjoy the last comfortable days before winter arrives. But there is nothing amusing about being shut out of a country that we were looking forward to seeing and -just perhaps - becoming two of the 600+ non-resident citizens of the tiny micronation. I walk slowly around the barbed-wire fence, circling the country in about 45 seconds; within the nation's boundary is a single, wooden ball-shaped house: the only building in the sovereign state, serving as its government center and, at one time, the residence of its founder and president.

Micronations exist. They dot the world in some of the most preposterous locations. They may be whimsical or purpose-driven; they may be the size of a small park or, well...a house; and they usually print their own passports, currency, and postage stamps. Some larger countries will even acknowledge, in their own acts of whimsy, the sovereignty of micronations within their boundaries. The city of Vienna has taken this action with Kugelmugel, after the entire country moved from Lower Austria in 1982 (it declared its independence in 1976, over a building permit dispute - guess what building?). Vienna now respects the existence of the Republic of Kugelmugel.

My own respect is tempered by the disappointment of having come all of this distance to discover that the country is closed. I prowl around the border like a frustrated tiger, becoming more aggravated by the minute. Fortunately, there is Connie to point out the obvious: "It's not going to open just because you growl at it." Grudgingly, I walk back toward the park's western edge. I am about to have more than my spirits lifted.

4.

"Look down there. Would it really mean anything if one of those dots stopped moving forever?"
- Orson Welles as Harry Lime in **The Third Man**

* * *

I am looking down at those "dots" - human beings - as Connie and I are standing in one of the small red cabins that rise to the top of the Wiener Riesenrad (Vienna Giant Ferris Wheel). Lime was right in one respect: the staggering height of the wheel dwarfs the people walking below, reducing them to specks and putting a knot in my throat as I realize how high I am.

I have a fear of heights; but I have a stronger need to ride this colossal beast that forms an iconic part of the Vienna skyline. Located in the Prater amusement grounds, this ride has held its number 3 slot on my Bucket List since I first watched *The Third Man*, a classic film set in post-WWII Vienna. It's a simple equation, really: *Favorite film + real-life location + public access = an insatiable drive to experience the site.* Even if this city had not been the capital of an empire, I would have found an excuse to come here just for the ferris wheel and the city's sewer system.

The Vienna sewer system - a major attraction? Yes. It's at number 4 on my travel wish list - another nod to the influence of a classic film. In the climax of *The Third Man*, the villain (Lime) is pursued by military police in a massive manhunt through the tunnels and stairways of an underground Vienna. The cavernous main branch of the sewer runs into the Danube, as a maze of smaller tunnels, passages, and canals fans out from the vaulted center and runs beneath the city. At some point, a clever entrepreneur latched onto the intense fan interest in the movie, and launched a guided tour of the parts of the sewer system that feature in the movie. Most movie buffs know about the tours; regular tourists tend to be ignorant of the activity just below their feet.

As the day grows overcast, we hustle to the other side of the city, south of the Ringstrasse. After some difficulty in finding the entrance site for the underground journey, we join a larger group of movie fans and don hardhats with flash lamps. We are ready. More than that, we are *psyched* (well, *I* am; Connie is more bemused by my enthusiasm than interested in spending part of her vacation in a sewer, but then she had her Greek cruise and I am getting my clammy underground tunnels - seems a fair trade to me). Our guide hauls up the triangular hatches that make up the circular cover to the stone stairs below.

It's starting to rain. The stairway spirals down several feet and leads us to one of the chambers that had featured in the film. Projections of scenes from the movie play along a wall, as the guide explains the job of the city workers. It is a fascinating contest as the guide tries to raise his voice above the roaring torrent of water crashing through the canal below. Soon we are passing through more tunnels, and we arrive at another large chamber. We are against the wall on one side, with a metal guard rail keeping us on the pathway. Beyond the rail, the chamber drops straight down into a canal fed by a waterfall running the length of the chamber opposite us. This drop has a mild flow of water, and in the film, characters are able to walk along the top of the waterfall.

But something is amiss. We can hear the intensity of the rain outside increasing; we can see the waterfall surging with power, forcefully filling the canal below, which starts to rise. And at the other end of the pathway, our guide and one of the sewer workers are engaged in a heated discussion that the guide is obviously losing. With a helpless shrug, we are told that we must return to the surface; the storm above is rapidly filling the sewer with runoff. The nervous tenor in our guide's voice - along with his annoyance - strikes fear into us. We don't panic, but there is now an urgency about our passage to the stairs up to the street.

Connie and I cross the adjoining boulevard to enter a corner café. There, cradling a hot tea, I reflect on an experience that was a bit more of an adventure than I had anticipated.

5.

Schnitzel, schnitzel everywhere, and not a bite to eat. I feel like the landlocked version of the Ancient Mariner, trapped in a paradise of culinary temptations that I cannot indulge. Forbidden by my doctor from eating any meats or poultry, I find that there are only so many ways that a salmon filet can be made appealing.

So thank God for the hotel concierge - that master of the bottomless pit of city information. At the Hotel Capricorno, the keeper of cultural and culinary knowledge directs us to the streets behind the hotel - going away from the Ring - where he feels certain that we will find the gastronomic delights that we seek. He is correct. At the Biem Czaak, where the menu shows photos of their fare without translation, we choose two meals that we will share in a mix-and-match fashion that tickles our taste buds. What are we eating? Who cares - this is why we travel around the world: to explore new sensations, new ways of preparing foods that we'll rarely experience again.

The following evening finds us in La Lavante, seated at an indoor table surrounded by the smell of tobacco and wines - a heady experience that helps to negate the claustrophobic squeeze of tables so close together that chairs from one clash with the backs of others and nobody seems to mind. I order spaghetti with shrimp and salmon (I know, but…it tastes *so* good); and as my meal arrives, Connie and I dig in. A rosé wine complements the dish perfectly.

After the meal, we order more wine. The atmosphere becomes a pleasant blur, closing in and then expanding, as if the café itself is breathing rhythmically. For a brief moment, we are one with the establishment - the tables and chairs, the diners, the revelers at the small bar just feet from our table; then we move, in what seems a gliding motion to the door. The brisk night air hits us, and sobers us just enough to enjoy a leisurely stroll back to the hotel. As we head to the elevator, I give a thumbs-up to the concierge; he smiles almost imperceptibly, and nods.

6.

Viennese days in autumn have a pattern about them. A crisp sunny morning leads into a slightly overcast early afternoon that subtly suggests the possibility of rain sometime soon. A light drizzle or a short deluge may ensue, or, after teasing the visitor with the threat of a downpour, the clouds may part and reveal a brilliant sun. Whatever the outcome of a grey afternoon, it soon becomes apparent that any outdoor activity is best planned for the early hours.

So it is that we are heading on a bus toward the Schönbrunn Palace in the morning. The Palace is one of those "must-see" tourist spots - the ones that your traveling companions and your non-traveling friends at home will ostracize you for daring to miss. But Connie and I are museumed-out (after Rome, Athens, and Istanbul), and the Palace is, after all, just a 1440-room collection of art and furniture. Heresy!, I hear you say. Perhaps, but we're too jaded by this point to care. We just want to go and see the architecture and to walk around it for a while - and we mean "around" it, not in it - past beautiful gardens and immaculately groomed lawns that are rightfully world famous.

Schönbrunn Palace does have its history, however. Fenced off as a royal hunting ground, the eventual Habsburg owners built the palace over a period of centuries, reaching its current appearance around the 1740s. In 1830, Franz Joseph I was born here, and would use the palace as his seat of government. By the age of 18, he was the Emperor of Austria, and in 1867, having annexed Hungary, he became the Emperor of the Austro-Hungarian Empire.

By that time, the Empire consisted of the two major countries and a collection of contentious states such as Serbia and Bohemia. The Empire did not seek to expand and conquer; Franz Joseph spent much of his reign facing down anarchists and regional independence movements. Over a 45-year period, he mostly succeeded, but at terrible costs: his younger brother Maximillian - whom Franz had sent to Mexico to secure Habsburg holdings there - was executed in a rebellion; his son Rudolph, who was his chosen heir-apparent, committed suicide; his beloved wife Empress Elizabeth was assassinated by an anarchist while visiting Geneva, Switzerland; and his nephew and next pick as his successor, Archduke Franz Ferdinand, was gunned down in Sarajevo in 1914.

Franz Joseph I would die in the same building that had ushered him into the world. In 1916, he passed away in his beloved Schönbrunn Palace. The empire that he had ruled would only survive him by two years and one emperor (Karl I).

As anticipated, the clouds are rolling in. Connie and I head quickly for the parking lot - which takes up a large segment of ground in front of the palace, ruining its "regal" appearance from the road - to avoid the crush of tourists who are, already, moving *en masse* to their assigned buses. Fortunately, only a light shower drops over the city, and by the time we arrive at the Ringstrasse, a damp breeze blows under a sun just peeking through the haze.

7.

My wife loves animals, so it is an easy feat to convince her that we should spend some time visiting the Spanish Riding School in the heart of Vienna. A short stop turns into an afternoon of touring the school - its training paddock, its grand performance hall, and its stables - and marveling at the incredible beauty of the Lipizanner stallions. In their individual stalls, each horse has a unique personality that can be seen in their eyes and felt in the graceful movements of their coiled muscles - even in the confined spaces they inhabit when they are not training or performing.

The Habsburgs initially bred these beasts, using Arabian horses and the Spanish Lusitano breed, among others, to produce a line of horses that would be the pride of the Austrian military. After centuries of development, these stallions came close to extinction during the wars of the early 20th century. A team of American soldiers was sent into Austria during the Second World War to save them.

Our tour begins with a stroll past the training paddock and into a courtyard where one of the white stallions pokes his head out of a wooden stall. The guide, while admonishing us to refrain from taking photos, suddenly "relents," and allows us to "sneak" a few pictures because we're being such good guests. The action is so practiced that I suspect each group will turn out to be worthy of the transgression as they parade through the school.

Then it's into the stables to see the dozen or so white

horses. They are not really white; most are grey, and some are darker. But all have a white coat of hair overlaying their skin. And that, frankly, is all that is needed to put on a truly spectacular show of gleaming white stallions performing at the peak of their skills.

Leaving the school, I am amazed that no sounds escape into the streets that would betray the existence of horses and their stables and training grounds in the heart of this modern metropolis. The institution is invisible amongst the cosmopolitan bustle of the city.

8.

Vienna's mornings are created for casual strolls, and we walk along the eastern and southern Ringstrasse with a slight sadness in our hearts, knowing that our travels are coming to an end. We have followed the course of empire through Europe, and we come to the final act with an unexpected joy at finding not just ruins, but communities of people who have welcomed us into their lands and who have opened their cities and their hearts to us.

The last tragedy that befell Emperor Franz Joseph - the assassination of the Archduke in Sarajevo in 1914 - led to the Austro-Hungarian Empire's involvement in World War I. The conflict that the generals thought would expand the empire and strengthen its world position instead destroyed it. With the dissolution of Austria-Hungary in 1918 by the Allies, along with the occupation of the Ottoman Empire in the same year, the age of imperial empire was a thing of the past.

The Vienna Opera House now looms before us,

wedding the grandeur of older times with the opulence and hope of the modern era. A block behind it, the Hotel Sacher welcomes travelers from around the world with the aroma of their famous Sacher Torte. Down the road, another walking tour is wending its way through the Old Town.

This is Vienna today. The sun floods the morning, the buildings glisten, the trams clang. And Connie and I walk arm-in-arm along the boulevard, strolling through time and history.

AND IN THE END: PARIS AGAIN

1.

The bitter cold of late October whips through Paris. Taking momentary refuge from the chill, Connie and I head into Les Invalides - and appropriately enough, begin our 3-day stay in the city by viewing the sarcophagus of Napoleon. The porphyry stone of the tomb shimmers as we circle it from above; below, others roam around the late emperor's final resting place in the subterranean level. We all stand beneath the huge dome covering the beginning and the end of the First French Empire - Napoleon himself.

It took some doing to get the British, in whose captivity Napoleon died, to allow the former emperor's body to be returned to France. But by 1840, the French monarchy was secure, and Napoleon's supporters were either long dead or too old to inspire rebellion.

Imperial empire is gone; Napoleon's sarcophagus may just as well hold *its* remains.

2.

Paris, for us, also means family. Connie's sister and her husband have been residents here for decades. While the days are spent visiting familiar sights - although, to my surprise, Connie, a musician, has never been to the Paris Opera House - the evenings are reserved for family.

Our first night, of course, is spent at Jennifer's apartment, enjoying a home-cooked meal and catching up on the past year's events. The following evening, we head to the Latin Quarter, where, in a small 17th-century church set back from a side road, we attend a concert for an up-and-coming violinist. The church, illuminated by dozens of candles, has perfect acoustics for the performance; for the next hour, we sit entranced by the young lady's skill.

As we leave the church, the October chill smacks our faces. We walk briskly for a few blocks, and find ourselves hustling into Bonventure, a corner café/restaurant about which Jennifer has heard good things. She is right; meals are simple but delicious, and we lose our time eating and talking through the evening.

Our final night finds us in the same restaurant that Connie and I (with my daughter Stephanie) patronized on our first night in Paris together in 2015. Just a short walk from our hotel, and a block from Jennifer and Stephane's place, bright lights flood the corner eatery, and the warmth, after coming from the street, wraps itself around the four of us. Our hosts have indulged their appetites here many times, and their recommendations are spot-on. Glasses of wine fill the gaps between courses, and more wine and conversation let time slip by quickly and without notice.

We make our goodbyes; and, in the matchbook of a hotel room that is costing us a small fortune each night, we pack for our flight home.

3.

Travel and history are the cranks that get my emotional and creative juices going. Combining the two, as we did this time (and for a month running), is a form of nirvana that remains one of my most cherished memories - and prods me to ask myself, "Where next?".

That answer remains elusive until a place triggers that latent but always potent desire to pick up and go; until that place connects to another place, and another; until I have an itinerary that won't be denied.

And then, Connie and I are off.

ABOUT THE AUTHOR

Wesley R. Mullen is a graduate of Archmere Academy in Claymont, Delaware, and of Villanova University. After working as a paralegal and a real estate agent in Philadelphia, Mr. Mullen spent 17 years with TV Guide as an editor/writer before moving to Florida, where he now lives with his wife Connie. Separately and together, they have traveled throughout Europe over the past 50 years.

Mr Mullen's first book of travel essays, <u>Thrilling Cities, Too</u>, was published in 2014. Since then, he has published four additional books of travel essays and a "memoir in essays."

If you have enjoyed this current collection of essays, please feel free to review or rate it.

**OTHER WORKS BY
WESLEY R. MULLEN**

Thrilling Cities, Too

Destinations: Café Hours

Destinations: Ship Leaves Harbor

Flaneur in a Porkpie Hat

When I Grow Up, I Wanna Be Kenneth Tobey!

Made in the USA
Monee, IL
14 November 2020